# Self-HYPNOSIS
## REVOLUTION

## The Amazingly Simple Way to Use Self-Hypnosis to Change Your Life

# FORBES ROBBINS BLAIR

 SOURCEBOOKS, INC.®
NAPERVILLE, ILLINOIS

This book is not intended as a substitute for medical advice from a qualified physician. The intent of this book is to provide accurate general information in regard to the subject matter covered. If medical advice or other expert help is needed the services of an appropriate medical professional should be sought.

Published by Sourcebooks, Inc.
P.O. Box 4410, Naperville, Illinois 60567-4410
(630) 961-3900
Fax: (630) 961-2168
www.sourcebooks.com

Library of Congress Cataloging-in-Publication Data

Blair, Forbes Robbins.
  Self-hypnosis revolution : the amazingly simple way to turn everything you do into power and fun / Forbes Robbins Blair.
      p. cm.
  Includes index.
  ISBN-13: 978-1-4022-0670-2
  ISBN-10: 1-4022-0670-4
  1. Autogenic training.  I. Title.

RC499.A8B565 2007
615.8'5122—dc22

                                        2006037111

Printed and bound in the Untited States of America.
VP 10 9 8 7 6 5 4 3 2 1

# Dedication

---

This work is dedicated with loving appreciation to Reverend Ann Davies and Clark and Dei Wilkerson—for the inspiration and insight they left behind.

# Contents

# Acknowledgments

Grateful acknowledgment is made to the following people and organizations:

Deb Werksman, editor, and the staff of Sourcebooks—for believing in the insight this book reveals. Carole Abel, literary agent—for presenting this work to the publisher and for her continued negotiation skills. Robert Morrison—for his literary expertise, time, and assistance on this project. Carrol Ann Chaiken, gifted intuitive counselor—for predicting the publication of this book. Dream Catchers—for their input, excitement, and encouragement. Kristin Cooper, sister—for her faith in me and my projects. Hilma Robbins Blair, mother—for her love and support. Alona Hapey, Joe Puhzchl, and Veronika Fox, coworkers and friends—who contributed, perhaps without realizing it. Teresa Thomas and Mike Albano, friends—whose comments added to the richness of the message of this work.

# Preface

**H**ave you ever wondered why most self-improvement programs fail to produce the life-changing results they promise?

I have.

And I've come to the conclusion that most self-help methods are too complicated, take too much time, and many of them are just downright boring.

I'm sure you already know that there are hundreds of ways to seek self-improvement. And there are just as many experts with techniques who can help you in that quest. In fact, there are so many that the choices are overwhelming. To pursue them all would take several life-times. Even to pursue a few takes commitment, time, and usually money—sometimes a great deal of money. What's worse is that often-times, even after much ado, there is little improvement to show for one's efforts.

I recently talked to a self-improvement enthusiast who had gone to a very expensive seminar featuring a well-known motivational speaker who promises people success, primarily in the area of career and finances. This highly charismatic speaker (and way too gifted salesman) reveals to his audiences relatively workable techniques, most of which he gleaned from other experts. And the feverish excitement stirred up at his seminars cannot be discounted for its motivational (albeit short-lived) effects. Anyway, the enthusiast extolled the virtues of the speaker along with the expert advice and techniques he disclosed. But upon closer inquiry I uncovered three disturbing things. One, this financially struggling gentleman had gone to the same costly seminar three times to the tune of thousands of dollars. Three times! Thousands of dollars! Two, the man confessed that his life had not changed in any noticeable way. Three, the man did not regularly practice any of the techniques that were taught. Not even one. It seems the only thing the man had after many hours and dollars spent was misplaced enthusiasm and self-delusion. His ego wouldn't permit him to admit to me or to himself that the whole thing was a bust.

It was sad.

Ultimately, I guess I can't blame the speaker, no matter how much money the seminars cost—not to mention the expensive "back of the room" books, CDs, and DVDs for sale…not that there's anything wrong with that. It seems that I must put the onus on the man who failed to put the techniques he learned to regular use. Yet the problem with so many self-help techniques is that they require a lot of commitment and substantial windows of time. And when push comes to shove, most people just aren't willing or able to give things ample time to work. They quit before receiving the promised benefit because there just isn't time to implement complicated strategies or, more likely, they just get bored. Frequently they never even put the techniques they've learned into practice at all. As a self-help enthusiast, I've been guilty of this myself. Not long ago I read a marvelous approach to mediation full of inspired methods. But there were so many steps and techniques that the road to mastery seemed long. I felt overwhelmed, and as a result I didn't put even one technique into practice. Again, I can't blame the writer. His methods and intentions were good—even inspired. It's my own fault. And yet, can I blame myself for not putting work into techniques that require more time and effort than I can logically afford? Perhaps my intuitive hesitation is a way of saving myself a lot of time.

## Solving the Self-Help Quandary

Maybe this is your first self-improvement book. Or perhaps you've read others. Many, if not most of them, can add to the quality of your life when you follow their prescriptions. Yet there's a basic problem with almost all self-help methods—they're complicated and take effort and time to put into practice. *And you just don't have the time!*

Sure, you'd like to spend an hour in daily meditation, but who's going to feed the kids their breakfast? And yes, you'd *like* to stand in front of the mirror and repeat positive affirmations over and over, but that will make you late for work. You'd love to go to a weekend seminar to see your favorite self-help guru, but your cousins are coming for a visit that weekend. You even record your favorite self-help show from television, but there's just no time to watch it. Oh well, that's life.

On the other hand, maybe you already spend allotted time putting other self-help methods into practice and you'd like to do more. But there's no room left in your self-improvement schedule to add yet another technique, and you don't want to sacrifice the programs you're currently using.

If only there was a simple way to promote self-improvement and change that didn't require any extra time out of your busy schedule—a way to advance and motivate yourself physically, mentally, and emotionally without slowing you down. Of course that seems impossible. Can there ever be a self-help method that doesn't demand any extra time to put it into practice?

Yes, there is!

Self-Hypnosis Revolution reveals an amazing self-improvement method that can be used in the midst of your busy life and therefore requires virtually no time commitment. Using the insights and simple techniques found in this book will help you:

xii Self-Hypnosis Revolution

- Improve or sustain your physical health
- Develop a clear mind and positive outlook
- Lead you toward opportunities for wealth and success
- Enhance your relationships and develop new ones
- Strengthen your spirituality
- Discover meaning and purpose in your everyday life
- And much more

You practice this simple yet powerful method not by sequestering yourself for minutes or hours, but as you go about your daily routine. You can use it while you take out the garbage, brush the dog, drive to the store, clean up the house, or during just about any other activity. As a matter of fact, the little everyday tasks like these are what make this secret method of self-change work.

You may be wondering how and why everyday tasks like taking out the garbage can be used as part of a self-help program. But that's what makes using Self-Hypnosis Revolution so much fun, because you'll learn that just about everything you do in daily life has the potential to help you improve, heal, change, and grow.

Once you understand the premise of this book, you'll see the revealed method as one of the simplest forms of self-therapy ever devised. And guess what? It's actually fun to do. So you'll have a tool that you won't just use for a week or two and then stop. You'll use it for the rest of your life.

Interested? Then come on! You're only minutes away from learning how to put Self-Hypnosis Revolution to work for you.

# Introduction

Self-Hypnosis Revolution is all about a discovery I made: that the self-improvement benefits of self-hypnosis can be achieved without the use of altered states—that there's a remarkably simple and revolutionary way to use everyday tasks to produce outstanding changes in motivation and behavior.

You might think, as many people do, that life is full of meaningless tasks. But I've discovered that the things you do every day are loaded with significance that can change your life and support your goals.

**Everything you do has an underlying meaning that provides an opportunity to plant seeds within your mind to promote healing, change, and growth.**

Every physical task, no matter how seemingly small or ordinary, contains life-changing symbolism for those with eyes to see it. By recognizing the significance of your workaday chores, virtually anything you do can be used to promote change and self-improvement for specific areas of your life, such as your health, career, spiritual path, and relationships. Imagine that…

- Every time you take a shower, you can rid yourself of negative emotions like fear, anger, and resentment.
- Whenever you eat, you can nourish and stimulate your mind as well as your body.

- As you drive your car to work, you can get closer to your career and financial goals.

This book unmasks the hidden, deeper meanings of dozens of everyday activities and teaches you how to use them to change your life. With Self-Hypnosis Revolution, daily chores and responsibilities suddenly become potent opportunities for change and true self-empowerment.

I don't mean to imply that in an instant all of your problems are going to be solved. You know that's not realistic. But you will be able to put this secret method to work during any activity at any time of day or night, and it will take no extra time out of your day. And by using this method repeatedly, you will find your life changing in beneficial and practical ways.

## A Different Way of Thinking

Self-Hypnosis Revolution will get you to think in a totally different way about self-hypnosis and your everyday life. In the beginning you might use this book in perhaps a plodding and more formal way, but after a while you'll find yourself going beyond the text and automatically recognizing the underlying value of routine activities as you go about them—and using them to transmute your mind, your body, and other important areas of your life. And when you do this, suddenly those very tasks, instead of causing drudgery, turn into tools for self-transformation. You will actually look forward to cleaning out the bathtub, brushing the dog, or paying bills.

Hard to believe, but true.

In Self-Hypnosis Revolution, you will be shown how to turn even the simplest of mundane tasks into powerful, symbolic gestures that impress potent messages upon your inner mind. You'll also begin to understand that personal growth and change needn't be confined to the meditation chamber or sought in the words of today's self-help gurus. The power is yours, today.

## Not Your Papa's Self-Hypnosis

Self-Hypnosis Revolution broadens the traditional scope and definition of self-hypnosis. When you think of self-hypnosis, you probably think of setting aside ample time for application, the induction of relaxation and trance state, along with the application of hypnotic suggestions. Many standard hypnotic suggestions use imagery and metaphors that require visualization on the part of the practitioner. And while I am a hearty supporter of traditional hypnosis and self-hypnosis, the method in Self-Hypnosis Revolution is different because it requires...

- No time set aside for application
- No relaxation state or trance of any kind
- No visualization ability

Having read that, you may wonder whether Self-Hypnosis Revolution is hypnosis at all. And I'll grant that the concepts of Self-Hypnosis Revolution are unconventional, but definitely related to hypnotic theory. The relationship between traditional self-hypnosis and Self-Hypnosis Revolution is that both utilize the power of suggestion and metaphor to communicate with the inner mind in order to elicit deep change. In the book, I discuss this relationship in more detail so you can begin to understand why this new concept warrants the word *revolution*.

## Steeped in Metaphor

You may notice at some point that the text of this book is laced with metaphors used in everyday language. Some of them are so common they are considered clichés. I write this way on purpose to impress on you, whether consciously or unconsciously, the familiarity and communicative value of symbolic imagery, which has a lot to do with the disclosed method. I do it to underscore that you are already steeped in the power of symbolic language and thinking, which are at the core of this book's premise. It will be, therefore, a small leap for you to begin using the metaphors of your everyday activities to communicate potent self-suggestion to your inner mind that can lead you to a happier, healthier life.

Did you count how many metaphors were in the previous paragraph?

Save that thought.

## How the Book Is Arranged

The first five chapters of the book discuss what Self-Hypnosis Revolution is and how to apply it. You'll discover how it compares to some related self-improvement techniques and what makes it so powerful and unique. You'll learn how the method works and be offered ready-to-go programs that you can start using today. You'll also learn how to create your own program and put it into practice.

Chapter 6 is a reference section and the core of the book. It is a compendium of the dozens of activities you can use for your self-improvement programs. It reveals the powerful meaning of your everyday tasks and contains information you'll use to understand and utilize the method and programs revealed in the other chapters.

Chapter 7 has additional information about using the techniques of Self-Hypnosis Revolution, and the two appendixes provide more readymade programs and multiple blank templates for composing your own custom-made programs.

## Fast and Easy Style

Putting Self-Hypnosis Revolution into practice is fun, and learning the concepts and basic program does not take long. If you've already read my book, *Instant Self-Hypnosis: How to Hypnotize Yourself with Your Eyes Open*, you know that I'm not long-winded. A primary advantage of using the method in Self-Hypnosis Revolution is that it saves you precious time. So I'm not going to waste your time with drawn-out treatises or case studies. That's not my style. My objective is to get you started with the basic method quickly. In fact:

**It's my goal for you to start using the basic method within approximately one hour from when you begin reading this book.**

I believe the ideas and techniques in this book will change the way you look at your everyday existence—forever. Once you understand the principles, you'll have a self-help method that can be put to use at virtually any moment of the day. And what I hope will happen over time is that you'll no longer need this book to put the method into practice. You'll start thinking differently about any activity, and you'll automatically realize its secret underlying significance and how that activity might apply to your life in a positive way.

# 1

# The Power of Self-Suggestion

Self-Hypnosis Revolution reveals an effective way to communicate with your inner mind to elicit positive change. In order for you to understand this unusual method, it is first important for you to understand the definition and importance of suggestion. In this chapter, we'll discuss the power and effect of suggestion and self-suggestion (how they're different and how they relate to each other). We'll take a look at the well-known practices that use the power of suggestion as forms of self-therapy and discover their strengths and weaknesses.

## Suggestion and Self-Suggestion

As a clinical hypnotherapist, I have long come to realize what an important role the power of suggestion plays in the choices we make and the quality of life we produce for ourselves. And while I'm sure you've heard of the power of suggestion, few people ever pause to think about what is meant by it. What is suggestion? And how and why is it considered to be a source of power? Here's my definition:

**A suggestion is an idea or proposal designed to elicit or affect a response in thought or behavior.**

These proposals come to us from a variety of sources and in varied ways. There are external suggestions, which can come from people, places, or things. Any time someone *asks* you to do something, it's a suggestion  Any time someone *commands* you to do something, it's simply a more emphatic suggestion: it's up to you to comply. For example, if your supervisor tells you to clean up the display case, it's really just a suggestion. If a bill comes in the mail with a demand for payment, it's really a suggestion with an underlying imperative. Another example of suggestion at work would be when you shop at the grocery store and you notice an appealing picture on the frozen pizza box. That picture is an external suggestion designed to influence (or seduce) you to purchase that item. External suggestions also come in the form of revealed information. Any time someone tells you something about himself or herself, you're exposed to suggestions. Anytime you read anything, you're exposed to suggestions. This book you're now reading is full of suggestions.

Self-suggestions, on the other hand, are ideas we propose to ourselves, ideas that initiate from our own minds. A good example of a self-suggestion would be when you ask yourself what you feel like eating for dinner. When you ask this of yourself, you quickly think about different foods or cuisines and you make a decision based purely on your tastes and internal motivations. Or to put it more simply, you talk yourself into choosing what to have for dinner. Your life is full of this kind of internal dialogue—or internal self-suggestion. You make suggestions to yourself every day, and this should be plain enough to see with a little bit of awareness.

## Your Mental Diet

Suggestions have a strong impact on your quality of life. I'm sure you've heard diet gurus say "you are what you eat." They are saying your physical condition is directly related to your diet. They contend that what your body digests and absorbs has a strong bearing on its ability to function. Suggestions, by analogy, are like food—food for the mind. And the suggestions you take in on a daily basis, whether from an external source or from self-suggestion, comprise what you might call your *mental* diet. Every idea you expose yourself to, whether coming from the media, your family and friends, or even self-talk, comprise your mental intake. And they can potentially have a serious impact on your emotions, mind, and body.

Suggestive thoughts can impact you as a result of sudden or repetitive events. But it's how you interpret them that matters. For instance, do you remember when you were last thrown a surprise party? Talk about sudden, huh? Or maybe when you heard the news about the latest bombing. What a shock. Each of these can affect you because of the thoughts they suggest and the emotions they can evoke in you. Recurring events can also affect you. Being told by your mate every day what a wonderful person you are will have a cumulative effect on your self-esteem. On the other hand, watching the negativity of TV news programs day after day can profoundly change how you approach the world.

Perhaps none of us can predict when sudden events may occur or how they'll affect us. But the predictable and repetitive events—those are the kind we can and should control. And it's up to us to decide what food for thought we're going to digest and what we'll discard. We should learn to control them because…

**Ideas we expose ourselves to on a regular basis shape who and what we are and what we believe about ourselves.**

## How Your Mental Diet Affects You

Your mental diet affects your psychic and physical well-being. It should be obvious that if you expose yourself to negativity your thoughts and emotions are affected. And if you do this on a regular basis, it is not hard to understand that you might be so deeply affected you can become consistently fearful, angry, and negative. This negativity can have a strong effect not only on your general outlook, but on your thoughts and feelings about specific areas of life, like career and relationships. Let's say you expose yourself to gossip about the divorces and new marriages of current celebrities. It might have a serious impact on the way you handle your relationships. That's the insidious effect of such gossip, and you may not even be conscious of it.

But it is more than just your mental health that is affected by your mental diet. Your body is also subject to the power of suggestion. You might wonder how your thoughts can affect your physical body, as many of us believe and act as though body and mind are separate. But the truth is…

**Every thought you think affects your physical body.**

Your mind is not an abstract island with a remote relationship to your body. They are inexorably linked. Are you surprised? When you think about a happy memory, your subconscious mind instructs your body to reproduce the physiological state associated with happiness, including the excretion of the feel-good hormones called *endorphins*. When you watch an action movie your heart races along with the hero's. When you read a suspense novel, your body reacts to what you are thinking to create the physiological manifestation of fear. We watch movies largely so we can vicariously experience the stories through the characters. But there *is* a physical consequence, because your subconscious stores all of your emotional and physiological reactions in its memory for future reference. This doesn't have to be a bad thing, of course. A lot of the New Thought crowd frown on watching a movie with thrills, adventure, and violence of any kind. But it can be argued that the mind can utilize information of a seemingly volatile nature in order to work through personal issues. And while I am not specifically advocating graphic violence in movies, books, or music, I am pointing out that it may well provide a means for some individuals to get in touch with deep inner conflicts and hopefully begin to resolve them.

I also want to make it clear that I'm not one of those gurus who will tell you never to think a negative thought or that you should be positive no matter what your mood or circumstances. I don't think that's realistic for most of us and I'm not even sure whether it's completely beneficial. Neither am I going to tell you what television shows you shouldn't watch or what songs you shouldn't listen to. Just as there's a place for junk food in many peoples' lives, thought junk food might have a purpose as well. It obviously fills some sort of need. The problem, though, is in consuming too much junk and not enough of the healthy stuff. Just as when we eat too much of the wrong foods we can expect illness and disease to catch up with us, this is also true with thought junk food. Failing to pay attention to our mental diet might lead to feeling "blue" or even a condition like neurosis or depression. It also could weaken the immune system, which might lead to illness. So it becomes crucial to find ways to supplement our mental nutrition. We must find a way to supply ourselves with healthful, uplifting suggestions to counteract the negative ones.

## Positive Self-Suggestion for Good Mental Nutrition

As briefly discussed, we all talk to ourselves whether we realize it or not. Some may actually talk aloud to themselves, which is perfectly natural and healthy according to most mental health experts. I do that sometimes. Others do it all in their heads. Regardless, all of us keep an internal dialogue going in which we tell ourselves about what we think about our lives, our values, and how we esteem ourselves. Self-talk is essentially synonymous with self-suggestion, and has a tremendous impact on how we feel about things, how we interpret events, and whether we are open to change. And self-suggestions—designed to support personal goals, emotional well-being, and bodily processes—provide a source of healthy mental nutrition.

Practicing positive self-suggestion is the mental equivalent of eating nutrient-packed vegetables on a regular basis. It not only uplifts the mind, but also helps counteract the mental junk food and negativism most of us are exposed to frequently. It also allows us to choose how we interpret the world around us: how we respond to life, rather than simply allowing our instincts to react for us. Additionally, it can actually be used to create new patterns of thought and behavior that can lead us to better mental and physical health and even lead us toward greater success in our relationships, careers, and spiritual aspirations.

## Self-Suggestion versus Positive Thinking

You may be thinking that all of this makes sense and is, in fact, somewhat obvious. After all, most of us have heard of positive thinking. And isn't positive thinking the same thing as positive self-suggestion?

No, it isn't.

While the two may be related, they are not the same. Positive thinking centers on purposefully and formally holding uplifting thoughts, especially amidst the obvious setbacks and chaos that life sometimes brings. It's a wonderful notion, but very difficult to pull off for most people, as it runs counter to emotional reactions we sometimes naturally have when experiencing unfortunate events. For many people, this author included, it somehow feels very false and draining to insist that all one's thoughts and emotions be happy ones and to attempt to drown or deny any negative ones. A friend of mine who once had aspirations to become a devoted Franciscan monk told me that a self-help book advised that he think only positive thoughts for one day. He confessed that by the end of that day he was completely exhausted, mentally and physically. Perhaps a Zen master finds it easy to be at peace no matter what apparent chaos is manifesting, but most of us, I think it's safe to say, are not Zen masters. So admitting to "ouch!" when it hurts is an understandable and healthy reaction to adverse circumstances and events.

Positive self-suggestion, on the other hand, is not an attempt to deny the sometimes harsh realities we may encounter. It is a way to simply move forward with what we *do* want for our lives. Or, to illustrate, upon falling down and scraping a knee the positive thinker might say, "My knee doesn't hurt. I feel just fine." Someone practicing self-suggestion, on the other hand, might say, "Ouch. I hurt my knee. I call upon all of my resources to help my knee heal quickly."

## The Key to Effective Self-Suggestion

The basis for success with any form of self-suggestion has to do with proper communication with the *subconscious*. The subconscious is the key to effective self-suggestion, so it's important that we have an understanding about some of its functions and faculties.

The subconscious (which some refer to as the *unconscious*) is that aspect or level of the mind below the threshold of your awareness. In other words, we are usually not aware of its thoughts or actions. It is responsible for running the thousands of autonomic bodily functions of the body, such as blood pressure, breathing, metabolism, etc. It is the repository for all memories and habit patterns. Additionally, it is the filter through which all perceptions must pass on the way to awareness. And while much is still unknown about the subconscious, some of the ways the subconscious operates have become apparent through observation. Here is a brief list:

*The subconscious is open to suggestions originating from the conscious level.* This part of the mind responds to directives coming from the conscious level and the truth is that we are giving directions and suggestions to it virtually all of the time, whether we know it or not. And the subconscious does not discriminate between good directives and bad ones. In a sense, it is rather like a computer in that whatever you put into it is what you will get out of it. The reason some of our intended ideas "stick" while others don't depends on whether there is a consistent and motivating emotion supporting them. The directions accompanied by strong emotions tend to get absorbed, while those that do not are often ignored. Many of our notions to change ourselves never "take" because they are contradicted by other ideas.

*The subconscious controls our bodily functions.* The subconscious not only runs the autonomic functions of the body, but also is actually the intelligence that builds and regulates our cells and controls our immune system. While the quality of air, water, nutrition, and medicine supply determine the raw materials we supply our bodies, it is actually the subconscious that makes intelligent use of them.

*The subconscious responds to repeated actions.* Real-world behaviors often make the greatest impact on the subconscious. Sporadic activity followed by inactivity makes a far lesser impact than a little done with great frequency and consistency. The subconscious tends to respond to the dominant image and emotion—to what or where we place the most attention and feeling.

*The subconscious responds to images and symbols.* Images act as strong suggestions to the subconscious, which for many people are far stronger than abstract words or concepts. Images, pictures, and symbols are a kind of shorthand communication for the subconscious.

## Methods of Self-Suggestion

As mentioned, all of us engage in self-suggestion on a regular basis, though we rarely stop to analyze it. For most people, the process is automatic and the results they get from it may be mixed, often due to conflicting messages they inadvertently give themselves. For instance, if I tell myself one moment that I love chocolate cake and the next moment I remind myself chocolate cake makes me fat, I send a conflicting message to my inner mind. My attitudes and behaviors regarding chocolate cake may then become understandably erratic, so a structured method for delivering consistent messages to the subconscious is needed. It allows me to gain conscious directed control over at least some of my self-communication.

There already exist several (more or less common) formal or structured methods of self-suggestion that have become popular in recent times. The goal of all formal methods of self-suggestion is to create a strong impression on the subconscious, because one thing is clear when it comes to self-communication:

**If the subconscious remains unimpressed by our communiqués, our current situation and patterns of thought and behavior are likely to stay the same.**

You may be familiar with several structured forms of self-suggestion.

Self-hypnosis is a technique utilized to quiet or bypass the mind's natural filter so relatively direct communication can take place between the conscious mind and the subconscious. In this state, suggestions for positive change are imparted from the conscious mind to the subconscious. Creative visualization is a technique requiring the participant to imagine specific and often metaphoric imagery to send messages and create an impact on the inner mind. This is usually performed in a very relaxed physical condition. Self-affirmations are positive statements about the self repeated over and over until their intention is absorbed by the subconscious. All three of these methods have their merits and drawbacks. Let's examine them briefly.

Traditional self-hypnosis is, indeed, a wonderful tool for self-improvement. And I've made it as easy as possible to utilize in my book, *Instant Self-Hypnosis: How to Hypnotize Yourself with Your Eyes Open*. But not everyone is excited or comfortable with the whole *altered states of consciousness* thing, and it does take practice and at least fifteen minutes to perform, which can be a challenge to those with a difficult schedule.

Creative visualization, likewise, can be a marvelous tool for change. But many people (if not most) find it difficult or impossible to visualize to any great extent, so the potential power of the metaphorical imagery is lost on them. It should also be noted that if performed in a relaxed state, as it frequently is, this form of self-suggestion is really a form of self-hypnosis in disguise. And again, many people aren't comfortable with that or simply don't have the time.

Self-affirmations are a great idea on the surface and require no altered state on the part of the practitioner. In actual practice, however, problems are typically encountered. For one, the results are usually slow in coming and it takes quite a bit of time and effort to repeat phrases dozens of times, day after day. The idea of using regular repetition to saturate the subconscious is a valid and powerful one, but it often produces a state of boredom in the practitioner. And affirmations delivered in a state of boredom are very likely to be ignored by the subconscious. Also, as with creative visualization, when self-affirmations are performed in a relaxed state, it becomes a form of self-hypnosis, which then owes its effects primarily to the altered state.

## The Ideal Self-Suggestion Method

From the aforementioned methods, we can put together components needed for an ideal method of self-suggestion provided that it requires neither an altered state of awareness nor any extra time to put into practice, yet retains the powerful elements of traditional self-hypnosis, visualization, and affirmations. Such a method would include:

*Frequency of application.* We know that the subconscious responds to regular actions and thoughts much more readily than to the sporadic. So it is vital that our self-suggestion efforts be persistent and consistent.

*Evocation of strong and positive emotions.* The subconscious responds well to self-suggestion when accompanied by honest and pertinent emotions. By positive emotion, I mean the generated feelings must focus on the good that you do want, rather than the bad or negative feelings that you may be trying to get away from.

*Utilization of appropriate images and metaphors.* The old saying "a picture is worth a thousand words" applies tenfold when it comes to communicating effectively with the subconscious. Mere mechanical words without assigned imagery have little impact on getting through. But by combining our words with suitable symbols, metaphors, and images, our intended directives are fully understood by the subconscious.

The big question after reviewing all of these ideal elements is: Can such an ideal method of self-suggestion be devised?

Yes! I call it Self-Hypnosis Revolution. But before I introduce you to this unique method in the next chapter, I want to make you aware of the number one requirement for the efficacy of any overt method of self-suggestion, including the one you're about to learn:

**You must believe in the power of self-suggestion for it to work well.**

That is to say, you must wholeheartedly believe that your subconscious is ready and willing to listen to and act upon your positive self-suggestions in whatever form you choose to utilize them. Further, you must understand that the subconscious is then more than capable of altering your body, your behavior, and even your circumstances to create and support health, happiness, prosperity, and so forth. Even a slight disbelief or skepticism in the value of self-suggestion or the powers of the subconscious can be enough to act as a counter-suggestion that can prevent your success.

Please recognize it is not that belief itself makes a self-suggestion technique work well in the long term. But serious doubt or skepticism is a sure way to stop or retard the effects of self-suggestion. That's because doubt and skepticism are evidence of an inverted belief—a belief that self-suggestion efforts are of no value. And that kind of belief acts as a psychological barrier and actually prevents progress with any method of self-suggestion, no matter how powerful its potential. Hopefully, this chapter has given you logical reasons on which to base a strong belief in the potential power of self-suggestion. So if you're ready to change your life, let go of doubt and skepticism now and embrace the possibility that there's something real here to learn and that you can use it to change your life for the better, whether in expected or unexpected ways.

# 2

## Self-Hypnosis Revolution— Self-Hypnosis without Going into a Trance

This chapter introduces you to the foundation for a potent form of self-suggestion that can be used in everyday life and requires no trance induction. You will learn about how I discovered the technique, and you'll begin to realize how powerful your everyday activities really are.

### A "New" Method of Self-Suggestion

I am now going to tell you in more detail about the potent self-suggestion method I stumbled onto and developed. It utilizes the natural imagery found in everyday tasks as a way to communicate with the subconscious mind to improve specific areas of life. I call it Self-Hypnosis Revolution because this method contains many of the potent elements of other self-suggestion methods, especially those of self-hypnosis, while avoiding most of the drawbacks. It can easily be grafted into one's daily routine because it can be put into practice virtually anytime, anywhere, while doing just about anything. And over a period of days or weeks, the life-changing effects become cumulative and apparent. I can't claim the basic idea is new in the truest sense, because many people have used it in a limited or isolated fashion, perhaps for centuries now. But as far as I know, my extrapolation of the basic idea and the practical way I am presenting it is new. And I can honestly claim that the method is something I pieced together and learned to do on my own, and for that reason I feel ethically comfortable in presenting it to you as "my" idea.

The Self-Hypnosis Revolution method involves the process of identifying underlying or symbolic meanings of everyday tasks and formulating pertinent self-suggestions to accompany those tasks. This may sound silly, strange, or complicated, but it really isn't once you understand it fully. Let me tell you where some of the insight came from for developing this method, as that will go a long way toward explaining its premise and concept.

Among my areas of expertise is hypnotherapy and dream interpretation. That is, I hypnotize others for positive behavioral change, and I analyze dreams to help people see how their dreams relate to their waking lives. At first glance, you might think these two areas (hypnotherapy and dream analysis) unrelated, but in fact they are two sides of the same coin—or at least kissing cousins, because they both deal with communication with the subconscious.

In hypnotherapy, an attempt is made to impart to the subconscious mind of the hypnotized person suggestions for positive change. These suggestions may be of a very direct sort such as, "You are now a non-smoker," or they may be of a more subtle variety such as in the use of analogies and metaphors like, "You feel as calm and peaceful as a quiet mountain lake."

In dream interpretation, the basic objective is to take dream images and match their associations to the things that are happening in real life. Often a dream will present metaphors for waking events, and will also reflect thoughts and feelings about those events. For instance, to analyze a dream about a storm, I first consider what storms can metaphorically represent. Since storms are associated with danger, violence, or trouble, I might ask the dreamer whether there is any turbulent trouble occurring during waking life, or whether the dreamer feels angry about something. You see how it works? A dream about a storm is rarely about actual weather conditions. Instead, the mind manufactures moving images of a storm as a symbolic expression for the way the mind is processing daily life. It is in the learning and sorting out of these associations of various images that a dream analyst's worth largely depends.

One day I asked myself, "If the dream images of common activities are symbolic for life issues and inner processes, could those same everyday activities be used in waking life to communicate to the subconscious effective suggestions for self-improvement?" And as a hypnotherapist who frequently uses metaphors to elicit change in my subjects, I instantly knew the answer to my question—yes, of course.

I went on and pondered that a dream about taking a shower is often symbolic for discarding unwanted thoughts and feelings. As a hypnotherapist, I have often had clients visualize this while hypnotized to help them shed negativity, because the subconscious mind understands the language of metaphor, which is (by no coincidence) a primary language or common tongue, you might say, of dreams. So I reasoned that I could make use of the real-life activity of taking a shower as a symbolic communiqué to my subconscious mind to help me let go of negative thoughts and emotions. I loved the idea, because I wouldn't have to put aside time to creatively visualize or hypnotize myself to receive the benefit. All I had to do was affirm the intention to release negativity while I was taking a shower. The idea intrigued me, so I decided to experiment.

I began my daily showers by giving myself the suggestion, "I cleanse myself of all negative thoughts and feelings." As the water washed over my body, I simultaneously imagined the water purifying my mind, sending all fear, anger, sorrow, jealousy, and greed down the drain. I ended each shower by generating a sense of mental and emotional hygiene. And I repeated this little ritual every time I took a shower. And in all honesty, I still do to this day.

At first I felt no significant change, but after about three weeks I began to notice that I was less riddled with negative feelings about myself, my life, and others. I grew less prone to outbursts of anger and frustration, and my words and actions toward others became kinder. My experiment was paying off. The act of taking a shower became for me a symbolic, moving gesture to communicate to my subconscious that I wanted to release unwanted feelings and thoughts. I knew then I'd made an important discovery:

**I found a way to take naturally occurring metaphors found in an everyday task and combine them with self-suggestion to produce an outstanding method of self-improvement without going into a trance.**

Once the shower experiment had proven successful, I began using the basic idea with other mundane activities. Taking out the garbage became a time to *throw out* old and useless ways of doing things. Driving to work became a way to direct my mind to become *driven* to succeed with my career plans. Petting the cat became a way to nurture or *stroke* my natural instincts.

**I began to realize that there is potential life-changing symbolism in virtually *every* activity of life.**

This method was and remains remarkably simple. It's just a matter of figuring out the symbolic value of an activity, matching it to an intention for self-improvement, and composing a phrase to accompany it. And because of my background in dreams and hypnosis, this was a relatively easy thing for me to do.

## A Revolutionary Idea

After putting this into practice, I began to realize that I had formulated a self-help method that could benefit anyone. Self-Hypnosis Revolution utilizes and combines components of potent self-improvement techniques, but in a unique way.

What I like best about this method is that it meets many of the criteria for effective self-suggestion while bypassing some of the problems with other methods. The method is put into practice right in the midst of everyday events, so no extra time is required. And because the method is performed during ordinary and oftentimes daily tasks, repetition occurs naturally. It requires no state of relaxation or trance of any kind. Further, it prominently utilizes symbolic and relevant imagery available in everyday life while requiring no visualization ability.

It is the combination of using self-suggestion with real-life tasks that makes this method particularly unique and potent. This is because actual tasks are not simply visual, as in a photograph, but are multisensory. For instance, taking a shower is not simply a visual experience, but also a tactile and auditory one. We not only see the water pouring down our bodies, but we also feel the water on our skin and hear the sounds it makes. And when an activity is coupled with a targeted self-suggestion, its multisensory message makes a strong impression on our subconscious that is unparalleled by affirmations, self-hypnosis, or creative visualization.

## The Symbolism in Everyday Things

The foundation of the Self-Hypnosis Revolution method lies in uncovering the symbolism found in everyday tasks. I acknowledge that not everyone has a background in dream symbolism or hypnotherapy. But I want to explain briefly how you can start identifying the symbolic meaning of seemingly trivial tasks. Once you get the idea, it is really quite easy and you'll never again look at mundane chores the same way.

Many years ago, a metaphysical teacher revealed to me that every activity in life is a sacrament. I didn't understand what she was talking about at the time, as my definition of *sacrament* was wrong. It brought to mind memories from childhood of people kneeling, eating bits of bread, and sipping grape juice in prayer. Eventually I realized that she meant an action or activity full of depth, meaning, and importance. And what she was saying is that everything in life contains a rich inner significance that should be recognized, cherished, and utilized. Once I developed Self-Hypnosis Revolution, I recognized she was right, because I learned…

**Every activity, even the most seemingly small or seemingly unimportant, has a deeper, symbolic meaning.**

Whether it's walking the dog, going to the store, or ironing clothes, everything we do has deep significance for us when we recognize its symbolic value. In a later chapter of this book, I offer you a substantial resource for grasping the hidden importance of common things. But it is my sincerest hope to show you that you needn't be dependent on this book to find those meanings. You can learn to see them all by yourself. It's really just a matter of thinking in a different way from which you are probably accustomed. You must learn to think metaphorically.

## Metaphors in Language

Even if you have forgotten grade school English, I assure you that you are quite familiar with metaphor. A metaphor is a way to use one thing to represent another thing: a symbol. We use a great deal of common metaphorical phrases and sayings, and they can demonstrate how easy it is to start identifying second meanings of everyday things. Here are a few common metaphorical idioms:

"Opportunity is knocking."

"An open-door policy."

"Living on easy street."

"The world is your oyster."

"As easy as pie."

"Step up to the plate."

"As good as gold."

"It's in the bag."

"A diamond in the rough."

"In hot water."

"In over your head."

"Nature is calling."

"A wake-up call."

"Hit the nail on the head."

Each of these examples illustrates the use of metaphor. When someone says they hear "opportunity knocking," we know they are speaking metaphorically and we know exactly what they mean. They are saying that opportunity is clearly and immediately available. It's the inner idea of knocking that correlates with availability. When someone has an "open-door policy," we know that has nothing to do with an actual door. It implies accessibility to communication. The door is used as a symbol for that which can be open or closed, just as communications between people can be open or shut down. When someone is told they need to "step up to the plate," we know that someone is being urged to take the initiative.

I have no doubt that you are familiar with most or all of the metaphorical phrases on the previous page and you do not need anyone to explain them to you. You undoubtedly use symbolic language frequently to communicate with others. The metaphorical images in such phrases provide a quick and vivid means for communicating an idea. You could even say...

**Metaphors are a kind of mental shorthand.**

And as you review the list above, you may discover such metaphors convey not only intellectual ideas, but emotional information as well. And it is due to their ability to convey or arouse emotions that metaphors provide such a potent means of communication. If you are able to understand the notion of metaphorical sayings in everyday language, then you are ready to grasp that every activity of life contains symbolism. Every little or big thing you do contains metaphors that can communicate with your subconscious to encourage positive changes in your body and mind. Let me give you a few examples of everyday activities and the useful metaphors they contain.

*Phone Calls.* A telephone is a communication device. Whenever you make or receive a phone call, you actively connect with whoever is on the other end of the line. So making a call represents making a connection with someone. It can even represent making a connection with some aspect of your own psyche. Every time you make or get a phone call, you can support good communication in your relationships or with your inner mind.

*Vacuuming.* A vacuum is a device that helps you clean and maintain floors and carpets. Floors are structures that give you something to walk on. They are an apt metaphor for anything that provides a foundation in your life. Vacuuming the floor, therefore, is a metaphor for purifying and maintaining whatever provides you with the basic foundation of life. This could apply, for example, to your beliefs, spiritual principles, or moral code.

*Traveling.* Travel is a physical means for getting from one place to another. It's symbolic for change or "movement" in your life. So whenever you travel, you have an opportunity to reinforce changes you wish to make in your body, your mind, your relationships, and so on.

Are you starting to get the idea?

It is not important whether you are instantly able to recognize the potential symbolism of everyday objects and activities, because this book does most of it for you. I'm just trying to get your wheels turning.

## Making the Mundane Meaningful

Your life is already rich with tasks that you can use to make you stronger, happier, and healthier. All you need to do is recognize it and start putting your wealth to good use.

I recently shared the concept of Self-Hypnosis Revolution with a longtime friend of mine who is a mother of three young children. Her time is dominated by taking care of her kids, her home, and her husband. She commented that she thought the method is particularly appealing to women in her situation, because it turns the endless and often thankless chores of cooking, cleaning, and driving the kids all over town into meaningful and fulfilling events. Using Self-Hypnosis Revolution, she can actually continue to serve and love her family while improving the quality of her own life at the same time.

I've also personally found this self-improvement method of great value when I find myself forced to perform some activity that I formerly found insignificant or "beneath me." For instance, before the publication of my first book I took a part-time retail position in a well-known, high-end department store to make ends meet. One day my manager asked me to polish the silverware on display. While I smiled and pretended to be happy to polish over one hundred pieces of silver, I inwardly thought, "Oh geez, is this what my life's come to?" But as I stood there with a polishing glove on my hand and began removing the tarnish off of every knife, fork, and spoon, I asked myself whether I could use the task to make a suggestion to my inner mind for personal improvement. I analyzed the objects and activities I was working with. I recognized silver as a collective symbol for the subconscious, which is the storehouse for my memories and behavioral patterns. Polishing tarnish from silver, I reasoned, is a metaphor for removing the natural negative thoughts that build up in daily life. It became clear that I was engaged in a profound and powerful metaphorical activity. So I quickly composed and silently repeated to myself as I continued to polish, "I cleanse my inner mind of the tarnish of accumulated negativity." The task I initially dreaded for its insignificance and drudgery was chock-full of personal meaning and value. I also found this realization actually encouraged me to concentrate on doing a good job on the task rather than a cursory one. My manager even commented on what a fine job I had done and subsequently asked me to do it again. But the second time around I was genuinely happy to oblige, for I knew I could send a powerful message to my inner mind while polishing silver. Yes, I actually looked forward to a task I would otherwise have found tedious. What a reversal in attitude this has caused in every area of my life. Things I used to consider unimportant have become a treasure trove of personal empowerment.

Your life is full of such hidden treasures—the undiscovered wealth found in the metaphors of your day-to-day tasks. A lot of people think they have to "get away from it all" to find a way to improve and enhance their lives. They believe an extended vacation to a foreign land is just the ticket for dramatic self-improvement. Yes, a vacation can refresh the body and mind. But without going anywhere special or spending another dime you can greatly enhance your quality of life every time you do ordinary things like talking on the phone, vacuuming the carpet, or driving to the store. Activities like these are *your* hidden treasures, and in the coming chapters I'll show you how to fully use your newfound pot of gold.

# 3

---

# The Self-Hypnosis Revolution Method—
# Four Simple Steps

From the previous chapters you have learned the value of suggestion and how everyday activities contain moving, symbolic imagery that can be used to create a strong impression on the inner mind for change. In this chapter you will be shown the basic way to apply this method to any activity and to your life.

## Four Simple Steps

Putting the method into practice isn't difficult—quite the contrary. If it seems complicated, boring, or burdensome, I can honestly say that you are doing it wrong. I've broken the method down into four steps to establish a formula for you to follow. Here they are:

### Step #1: *Select an ordinary activity.*

The first step is to choose an activity that you may wish to utilize for the method. It can be almost anything, but it is recommended that you choose an activity you perform on a regular basis. Ideally it should be something you do many times a week. Household chores and bathing regimes are prime choices for this method.

### Step #2: *Recognize basic associations of the activity.*

Next, think about the idea of the activity you selected, and off the top of your head consider what associations you might have with it. For example, what is bathing? It's a way to cleanse, purify, and release the body of accumulated dirt, bacteria, and debris. So our basic or "key" associations with showering include *purification* and *release.* Now consider the meaning and value of the associations made with the activity and how they apply to areas of life and self-improvement. In the case of bathing, it's easy to see the value, metaphorically speaking, of purifying certain areas of life and releasing what is unwanted. For instance, consider how important it might be to mental health, career, or relationships to release old habits or to purify and release accumulated anger and resentments.

### Step #3: *Compose and commit to memory a beneficial self-suggestion.*

In this step, first choose a targeted area of your life to improve, such as physical or mental wellness, career and finances, relationships or spirituality. Then, based on the value and meaning of the associations made with the activity, compose a single positive statement tailored toward improving life in that targeted area and memorize it. To illustrate the meaning and value of cleansing and release toward the improvement of physical health, you could compose a statement like, "I purify myself from all undesirable conditions and am perfectly healthy." If, on the other hand, you wish to target the improvement toward your relationships, you might change it to say, "I wash away all accumulated anger and resentment about those I care about."

### Step #4: *Recite the formulated suggestion as you perform the activity.*

As you begin the actual performance of your chosen activity, bring to mind the self-suggestion that you formulated. This may be done silently or out loud. Repeat it up to three times out loud or in your head. Think about what you are saying as you recite it.

After the recitation of your self-suggestion, continue on with the remainder of your task, whether it is short or long. Invest in your task with enthusiasm and fervor as you realize how it's communicating a powerful, living, moving suggestion that will certainly change your life in beneficial ways! Allow natural feelings of satisfaction and expectation to surface in your mind and body. Most of all, let yourself have fun with the task you selected now that you know what it will do for you. For example, after you've begun bathing and have recited the self-suggestion, cheerfully focus on the remainder of your bath. As you do so, keep in mind that the symbolic gesture of bathing along with the self-suggestion is communicating a strong message to the subconscious to purify accumulated negativity from your life.

That's it! Now all you have to do is to repeat steps 3 and 4 whenever you perform the activity. Whenever you naturally engage in the selected task, repeat the composed self-suggestion and then contemplate the significance of the activity as you continue to perform it. Continue this for seven days or until you've achieved your self-improvement goal to your satisfaction.

## Method Summary

1. Select an ordinary activity.
2. Recognize the basic associations of the activity and consider the meaning and value of the associations.
3. Compose and commit to memory a beneficial self-suggestion.
4. Recite the formulated suggestion as you perform the activity, focusing on the task as you contemplate its value and meaning.
   Repeat Step 4 whenever you perform the activity.

You can plug virtually any and every single thing you do into the formula above to make the method work for you. Give it a try. Pick an ordinary activity, and plug it into the four steps. It's actually enjoyable and turns your daily tasks into life-enhancing events. You may choose to just use one activity for the method or incorporate several to use throughout your day or week. By keeping the number of activities you use to no more than six, you'll prevent yourself from feeling over-loaded.

You might still be wondering which activities you may choose to uti-lize for this procedure. I realize you may be under-confident in your ability to figure out the key associations activities and to formulate good self-suggestions. The good news is that the bulk of the remain-der of this book is designed to take the guesswork out of it for you. There's an entire chapter devoted to activities, their meanings and associations, along with composed self-suggestions you can use to make your life better in many ways. But you should now understand the simplicity of the Self-Hypnosis Revolution method and how easy it is to put into practice.

# 4

## Ready-to-Go Programs to Break Bad Habits, Enhance Relationships, Improve Your Life, and Find Inner Peace

**U**nderstanding the basic method is easy enough, but putting it to practical use in an organized way is a different matter. While it's certainly possible to spontaneously put the formula to work during any activity, sporadic self-improvement efforts tend to get nominal results or fail entirely. Some sort of consistent plan of action and structure is necessary for most of us to ensure frequent application and good results. In this chapter you will learn how to use a basic program I've developed that gives you that plan and structure. You are also offered five ready-made programs so you can put what you learn to use as fast as possible.

### Program Overview

I developed Self-Hypnosis Revolution to be applicable to five major areas of life: the body, mind, career, relationships, and spirituality. The program first directs you to focus self-improvement on one of these five important and common areas of life. Next, a handful of commonplace activities are selected. These are activities you use throughout the program. A self-suggestion related to the area of improvement is assigned to each activity. The self-suggestions are recited, aloud or silently, whenever you naturally engage in one of the activities.

## The Five Target Areas

To start, first choose one of five particular areas of development, change, or improvement on which to focus for a seven-day period. The five areas are categories of life common to all of us, and just about anything you wish to improve about yourself will more than likely fall into one of them. To decide which area to work on, read through the descriptions below and select the area that is most suited to your current and most urgent need.

*Physical Wellness.* This area deals with all issues and problems of the physical body. It includes goals and desires for maintaining or improving bodily health, fitness, and beauty. Select this target area for goals that include...

- Improvement or restoration of an existing health condition
- Enhancement of personal appearance
- Increasing motivation to exercise, eat correctly, or to eliminate bad habits

*Mental Wellness.* This area includes issues of mind and emotions. Select this target area for goals that include...

- Reducing negativity and stress
- Increasing mental clarity and focus
- Enhancing memory
- Balancing emotional states

*Career and Finances.* This area includes issues of monetary supply as well as vocational concerns. Choose this target area for goals that include...

- Increasing monetary income
- Augmenting drive and aspirations for success

- Maintaining and controlling finances
- Developing new ideas for improved career and finances

*Relationships.* This area relates to your own beliefs, attitudes, and actions with or about other people. While we cannot and should not control the actions of those around us, we can affect our relationships by the quality of our own attitudes and projections. Select this target area for goals that include...

- Developing a loving attitude toward others
- Establishing and maintaining healthy relationships
- Fostering self-esteem in any relationship
- Setting personal boundaries with others

*Spirituality.* It has been estimated that over 90 percent of the world's population believes in a supreme being. Whether specified in a particular religion or simply seen as a grouping of guiding principles, this area deals with the health and empowerment of that which includes, yet extends beyond, standard physical or mental realms. Choose this target area for goals that include...

- Enhancing connection with the divine
- Affirming guiding beliefs and principles
- Stimulating spiritual growth and wisdom

## Selecting a Program Plan

At the end of this chapter are five programs prepared for your immediate use. They are ready-made planners that list and coordinate the information you need to apply your self-improvement program. In addition to getting you started quickly, the prepared program planners serve to introduce you to the way a program is structured.

This may be important in the event that you later decide to create your own programs as detailed in the next chapter.

There is one prepared program at the end of the chapter for each target area. There are five more available in appendix A near the end of the book as well. To select a prepared program, simply find the program planner that corresponds to the target area of your choice. For instance, if you've chosen physical wellness as your target area, then select the program planner that lists physical wellness as its target area.

## Understanding the Program Planner

Each prepared planner contains a list of activities, their key associations, and pertinent self-suggestions. Here is an explanation of the entries:

*Target Area.* This listing delineates on which one of the five target areas the program is centered.

*Start Date.* This heading is for entering the date you scheduled the program to begin. Writing a start date is a way of setting a specific commitment for your self-improvement program.

*End Date.* The date the program is scheduled for completion is noted here. A program lasts for seven days.

*Activity.* Because the prepared programs are designed for a broad range of people, the activities selected are those that are most common to all of us. Note that if for any reason there is an activity listed that is not a part of your regular life, simply omit it from the program.

*Key Associations.* Next to each activity listing are words that summarize the symbolic meanings of the task. While other associations may be drawn, the ones listed are considered "key" because they can be used toward self-improvement. In the compendium found in chapter 6, you will find an explanation for the deeper significance of the activities you'll utilize for your program.

*Self-Suggestions.* For each activity there is listed an accompanying self-suggestion relevant to the target area of improvement. These are the suggestions you recite as the activities are engaged.

## Using Your Program Planner

To put your program into practice, use the following steps:

1. Whenever you naturally undertake a task listed on the planner during the week, bring to mind (or read directly from your program planner) the key associations of the task and recite the self-suggestion that corresponds with that activity one to three times. The recitation should be out loud wherever possible. If it would be embarrassing or awkward to say it out loud, repeat the self-suggestion to yourself silently and carefully. Whether aloud or silently, recite the self-suggestion with clear intent. Think about the meaning of the self-suggestion and how it will feel when you have improved in your target area.

2. Focus on each activity as you perform it. Give it your full attention and care. Do it well and thoroughly. Enjoy it! Realize that the task sends a powerful message to your inner mind to improve your life in definite and noticeable ways. If you find your mind wandering from the activity, refocus it and bring to mind again the key associations affiliated with the task.

3. Consider, after the seven-day period, whether you want to continue with your program for another seven days or whether your results are satisfactory. Often times one week is enough to achieve noticeable or even outstanding results. Other times, it may take more than one week.

For your convenience, a reminder of the technique is posted on each prepared planner. At first, you may need to have your template handy so you can remember the key associations and self-suggestions from your list. I realized that this can be slightly awkward. But you will find that it pays off quickly, because in just a few days or repetitions of your daily routine, you will discover you automatically remember the key associations and self-suggestions. When that happens, you may no longer need to refer to the planner.

## Having Fun with Self-Hypnosis Revolution

One of the primary features of Self-Hypnosis Revolution is that it makes self-improvement enjoyable. So by all means have fun with your program. This enjoyment is not merely for entertainment value: it's actually important for the self-suggestions to work. Here's why:

**If using self-suggestion becomes a burden, the subconscious detects the emotional irritation, counteracting positive effects.**

With that in mind, it is important to never, at any time, become overwhelmed or irritated using the Self-Hypnosis Revolution method. If you're not in the mood to utilize the method as you undertake a task, skip it and do it next time. Or if doing a lot of self-suggestions throughout your day seems demanding, reduce the number of activities from your planner. It's far better to use only one or two activities with a fun and positive attitude than to use half a dozen with a sense of annoyance.

You may also find that you don't like the selected activities in the ready-made programs. If this is the case, create your own basic program taught in the next chapter, which allows you to handpick activities from the list found in chapter 6.

## Noticing and Tracking Results

It is helpful during and after every seven-day program to reflect on what changes have occurred. You may want to take notes as to any changes or progress you've noticed, whether great or small. Or, if there is no change at all, make a note of that too. Then you can decide whether you have achieved a satisfactory result. If you have not, you may wish to repeat your program or try another program.

The results from using Self-Hypnosis Revolution can be surprisingly quick and dramatic, though they are just as often gradual and subtle. In the latter case, it's important to give the method ample time to manifest in your life and to take notice when it occurs. Some personal circumstances and behavioral patterns, of course, may take quite a bit longer to change. But if you consistently use Self-Hypnosis Revolution, after about one to three weeks there are likely to be signs that the seeds of self-suggestion you've been planting are germinating, even in stubborn areas.

Sometimes the results will be obvious, such as the improvement of a physical health challenge, or the manifestation of a new job. Other times, the results may be subtle. You might feel a bit more outgoing, wake up looking forward to your day, or just have an increased sense of calm about life. Perhaps you might find that you argue less with those you love and have a better overall attitude. You could suddenly find you've changed some habit or longstanding behavior. I've personally encountered all of the above.

## More about Ready-to-Go Programs

The remaining pages of this chapter consist of the five ready-to-go programs available for your use. Again, please realize that the activities incorporated into these programs are those that are considered very common to all of us so they are applicable to just about anyone reading this book. For instance, virtually everyone needs to use the toilet on a daily basis. So that activity is included in one of the programs. But not everyone takes care of a pet, so that activity is not included in the prefabricated programs, even though it is found in the Compendium in Chapter 6. If an activity included on a prefabricated program is not one you perform regularly, omit it from your program.

You may desire to substitute other activities found in Chapter 6. The next chapter reveals how to create your own basic program, where *you* select the activities list.

## Program Planner
### Target Area: Physical Wellness
### Start Date:
### End Date:

| Activity | Key Associations | Self-Suggestion |
|---|---|---|
| 1. Awakening | Realization, recognition | "I awaken to opportunities to improve my physical well-being." |
| 2. Bathing | Purification, release | "I purify myself from all undesirable conditions and am perfectly healthy." |
| 3. Eating | Assimilation, thoughts, beliefs | "I assimilate every good nutrient that my body can use for optimum health " |
| 4. Paying Bills | Offering, atonement, responsibility | "I pay my body back with loving care for serving me well." |
| 5. Waiting (in traffic, in line) | Process, expectation, destiny | "I expect the natural processes of my body to bring and sustain perfect health." |
| 6. Getting the Mail | Receptivity, inner communication | "I am open and receptive to receiving messages from my body." |

*Do I want to continue this program for another seven-day cycle?*

_____yes _____no

Basic Technique Reminder

1. As you undertake each activity in daily life, review its key associations and recite with emotion the self-suggestion that corresponds with that activity.
2. Focus on each activity as you perform it while continuing to consider its key associations and symbolic meaning.
3. Perform the task with enthusiasm and interest, expecting positive changes in your life.

## Program Planner
**Target Area: Mental Wellness**
**Start Date:**
**End Date:**

| Activity | Key Associations | Self-Suggestion |
|---|---|---|
| **1. Arising** | Action, volition | "I take action in order to establish and maintain healthy thinking patterns." |
| **2. Communicating** | Understanding, information, rapport | "I establish and maintain excellent rapport with all levels of my mind for balance and well-being." |
| **3. Eating** | Assimilation, thoughts, beliefs | "I chew on thoughts and beliefs that uplift my mind and emotions." |
| **4. Cleaning** | Purification, order, maintenance | "I clean my thoughts of accumulated confusion and I restore order." |
| **5. Using the Toilet** | Release, elimination | "I let go of wasteful thoughts, beliefs, and behaviors." |
| **6. Sleeping (going to sleep)** | Restoration, processing | "I process all thoughts and emotions to create total mental wellness." |

*Do I want to continue this program for another seven-day cycle?*

____yes ____no

Basic Technique Reminder
1. As you undertake each activity in daily life, review its key associations and recite with emotion the self-suggestion that corresponds with that activity.
2. Focus on each activity as you perform it while continuing to consider its key associations and symbolic meaning.
3. Perform the task with enthusiasm and interest, expecting positive changes in your life.

**Program Planner**
**Target Area: Career and Finances**
**Start Date:**
**End Date:**

| Activity | Key Associations | Self-Suggestion |
|---|---|---|
| **1. Dressing** | Identity, self-image | "I identify myself as successful and allow others to see me that way." |
| **2. Grooming** | Beautification, presentation, preparation | "I groom myself for success and achievement." |
| **3. Unlocking a Door** | Gaining access | "I gain access to greater monetary supply." |
| **4. Driving** | Motivation, passion, self-control | "I drive myself closer and closer to success." |
| **5. Waiting (in traffic, in line)** | Process, expectation, destiny | "I wait for and recognize opportunities for increased prosperity." |
| **6. Shopping** | Searching, gathering, making choices | "I gather all of the appropriate information to make financial choices." |

*Do I want to continue this program for another seven-day cycle?*

_____ yes _____ no

Basic Technique Reminder

1. As you undertake each activity in daily life, review its key associations and recite with emotion the self-suggestion that corresponds with that activity.

2. Focus on each activity as you perform it while continuing to consider its key associations and symbolic meaning.

3. Perform the task with enthusiasm and interest, expecting positive changes in your life.

## Program Planner
**Target Area: Relationships**
**Start Date:**
**End Date:**

| Activity | Key Associations | Self-Suggestion |
|---|---|---|
| **1. Brushing Teeth** | Maintaining power | "I recognize my power to keep my relationships strong and healthy." |
| **2. Communicating** | Understanding, information, rapport | "I accurately communicate with others and establish mutual understanding." |
| **3. Crossing a Street** | Change, movement, transition | "I take the risks necessary to have wonderful relationships." |
| **4. Eating** | Assimilation, thoughts, beliefs | "I satisfy my appetite for loving and passionate relationships." |
| **5. Taking out the Trash** | Clearing, releasing, eliminating | "I throw out immature attitudes and behaviors to make my relationships healthier." |
| **6. Standing Up** | Recognition, self-assertion | "I stand up for myself in all of my relationships." |

*Do I want to continue this program for another seven-day cycle?*

_____yes _____no

Basic Technique Reminder
1. As you undertake each activity in daily life, review its key associations and recite with emotion the self-suggestion that corresponds with that activity.
2. Focus on each activity as you perform it while continuing to consider its key associations and symbolic meaning.
3. Perform the task with enthusiasm and interest, expecting positive changes in your life.

**Program Planner**
**Target Area: Spirituality**
**Start Date:**
**End Date:**

| Activity | Key Associations | Self-Suggestion |
|---|---|---|
| 1. Awakening | Realization, recognition | "I awaken to the love and presence of the divine in my life." |
| 2. Breathing | Assimilation, release, life | "The divine breathes life into me at every moment of my life." |
| 3. Drinking | Satisfaction, emotions, spirituality, purification | "I quench my thirst for spiritual knowledge." |
| 4. Climbing Stairs | Effort, achievement | "I ascend toward the divine one step at a time." |
| 5. Turning on a Light | Realization, knowledge, energy | "I recognize and access divine power and truth." |
| 6. Sleeping (going to sleep) | Restoration, processing | "I rest in the arms of the divine." |

*Do I want to continue this program for another seven day cycle?*

_____yes _ no

Basic Technique Reminder
1. As you undertake each activity in daily life, review its key associations and recite with emotion the self-suggestion that corresponds with that activity.
2. Focus on each activity as you perform it while continuing to consider its key associations and symbolic meaning.
3. Perform the task with enthusiasm and interest, expecting positive changes in your life.

# 5

## Create Your Own Program

In the previous chapter, you were offered prepared programs for your use. In this chapter you will learn how to create a program for yourself, so you can select your own activities and self-suggestions. You will use "Your Custom Program Planning Template" to create a program. The information and steps required to use a customized program are identical to those detailed in the previous chapter but are reiterated for your convenience.

### Customizing Your Program

A customized program works exactly the same way a ready-made one does. But with a customized program you choose your own activities. If you have been adventurous and looked at the Compendium found in Chapter 6 (see how well I know you?), you probably discovered that there are many activities available that do not appear on the ready-made programs. By creating your own program, you may select your own set of activities to use for your program according to your lifestyle. For instance, not everyone has to cook for themselves on a regular basis, so the activity of cooking is not included on any of the prefabricated programs. But perhaps you cook for yourself regularly, and would like to include it. By creating a customized program, you may select cooking as one of your activities with its corresponding associations and self-suggestions.

The customization process makes the programs more personal and potentially more effective than the ready-made kind. One reason is that the thought and attention required to create a program impresses upon the subconscious the importance of the endeavor. So creating a program in and of itself is a powerful self-suggestion to the psyche. Another reason is that the activities, selected to correspond to your particular lifestyle, may have more poignancy.

## Custom Program Planning Template Overview

Customizing a program requires filling out and using a form called Your Custom Program Planning Template. It looks much like the planners from the last chapter, except that none of the activities, key associations, or self-suggestions has been filled in yet. That's for you to do. You first choose the target area of self-improvement you desire. Then list on it up to six activities you intend to incorporate into your Self-Hypnosis Revolution program. You also list self-suggestions to go along with each task, suggestions corresponding to your target area. These self-suggestions are found in the Compendium in Chapter 6. Once filled out, your template acts as a reference and guide for putting your Self-Hypnosis Revolution program to use.

The following is an example of what a template looks like when it is completed. It looks very much like the ready-made programs, but is shown here for your convenience. Your choice of activities and self-suggestions will be different from those listed. After you review the sample template, an explanation of how this custom program was devised and utilized is offered, followed by instructions on how to fill out your own.

## Your Custom Program Planning Template (example)
**Target Area: Spirituality**
**Start Date: May 2**
**End Date: May 9**

| Activity | Key Associations | Self-Suggestion |
|---|---|---|
| 1. Awakening | Self-realization, self-recognition | "I awaken now to greater realization of myself and truth." |
| 2. Bathing | Purification, release | "I purify myself from all negative vibrations." |
| 3. Baby Care | Self-love, self-trust. | "The divine spirit loves, protects, and supports me unconditionally." |
| 4. Gardening | Nurturing, growing | "I grow and nurture inner wisdom." |
| 5. Cleaning | Purification, order, maintenance | "I purify and restore the beauty of my spiritual life." |
| 6. Climbing Stairs | Effort, achievement | "I take the steps required to reach the spiritual heights." |

*Do I want to continue this program for another seven-day cycle?*

_____yes _____no

## Template Explanation

The following is an explanation of the template entries.

*Target Area.* This heading is for listing which of five self-improvement areas will be focused on for the program. They are physical wellness, mental wellness, career and finances, relationships, and spirituality. Concentrate on only one target area during a single program.

*Start Date.* This heading is for entering the date you scheduled the program to begin. Writing a start date is a way of setting a specific commitment for your self-improvement program.

*End Date.* The date the program is scheduled for completion is noted here. A basic program lasts for seven days.

*Activity.* This heading is used to list one to six basic activities chosen from the Activities List.

*Key Associations.* This heading is for listing relevant symbolic associations of a listed activity. It acts as a reminder of the meaning and intention of the activities. These associations are found in the Compendium in Chapter 6.

*Self-Suggestion.* This heading is for listing the self-suggestions to be recited when the corresponding activity is performed. These self-suggestions are found in the Compendium in Chapter 6. The self-suggestion selected corresponds with both the chosen activity and target area. Though there may be more than one self-suggestion available, only one is chosen to be listed on the planning template.

## Setting Up Your Own Program

Now it's time to create your own program by filling out and utilizing Your Custom Program Planning Template. There is one included in this chapter. More blank templates may be found in Appendix B at the back of the book.

To create your program, take these steps:

1. *Choose a start date and an end date for your program and write them down on the planning template.* A seven-day program is recommended.

2. *Decide in what area of your life you most want change or improvement and write your decision in the Target Area space on the template.* In this book, we deal with five:

*Physical Wellness.* This key area includes goals for improving or maintaining body health, fitness, and beauty.

*Mental Wellness.* This area includes mental adeptness, clarity, and centered, happy, balanced emotions.

*Career and Finances.* This area includes issues of material and monetary supply and abundance, as well as those of seeking and maintaining a successful occupation.

*Relationships.* This area relates to your own beliefs, attitudes, and actions with or about other people. While we cannot and should not control the actions of those around us, we can affect our relationships by the quality of our own attitudes and projections.

*Spirituality.* This area deals with the health and empowerment of that which includes, and extends beyond, standard physical or mental realms.

3. *Choose activities for applying the Self-Hypnosis Revolution method.* To select activities you wish to use for your program, choose from the list in Chapter 6. You may choose as few as you wish, but do not exceed six for a program.

4. *Find the corresponding meaning and sample suggestion for each of your activities found in the Compendium in Chapter 6.* The next chapter has a compendium containing the activities listed along with key associations and detailed explanations regarding their symbolic value. Look up each of the activities you listed on your planner. Make sure you understand their relevance to your target area. Read the available self-suggestions. If there is more than one offered for your target area, notice which one is most applicable to your needs and circumstances. Sometimes there will be no self-suggestion offered for a particular activity, because its symbolism doesn't apply well enough to a particular area of life. In such a case, choose another activity for your program.

5 *Next to each activity on your template, write the corresponding key associations and one of the offered sample suggestions on the template.* Choose the self-suggestion from the Compendium based on the area of change you've selected to work on in your life and copy it onto your template. If more than one suggestion is offered in the reference, select the one you think would be most applicable to your needs.

## Your Custom Program Planning Template
**Target Area:**
**Start Date:**
**End Date:**

| Activity | Key Associations | Self-Suggestion |
|---|---|---|
| 1. | | |
| 2. | | |
| 3. | | |
| 4. | | |
| 5. | | |
| 6. | | |

*Do I want to continue this program for another seven-day cycle?*
    ____yes ____no

## Starting and Using Your Customized Program
Once you have filled out your Custom Program Planning Template, you are ready to start using your customized program beginning on your chosen start date. The procedure is identical to the one discussed in the previous chapter. Here is a refresher:

1 Whenever you naturally undertake a task you've listed on your planning template during the week, bring to mind (or read directly from your planning template) the key associations of the activity and recite the self-suggestion you chose to accompany that task up to three times. The recitation should be out loud wherever possible. If it would be embarrassing or awkward to say out loud, repeat the self-suggestion to yourself silently and carefully. Whether aloud or silently, recite the self-suggestion with clear intent and emotion.

2. Focus on each activity as you perform it. Give it your full attention and care. Do it well and thoroughly, whatever it is. Have fun with the task, realizing that it's sending a powerful message to your inner mind that will improve your life in definite ways. If you find your mind wandering from the task, gently refocus it, as you remind yourself of the key associations.

## Tips to Remember

During your program, remember that you may have to have your planner handy so you can recall and recite the self-suggestions at first. But after just a few days of repetition, you will automatically remember them and no longer need the planner. Also remember to have fun with your program as discussed in the previous chapter. If utilizing the full number of activities you've chosen feels burdensome at any time during the program, reduce the number of activities.

## After Your Program

After the completion of your seven-day customized program, it is time to evaluate whether you have completed your improvement goal to your satisfaction. If you haven't gotten adequate results then you may consider whether to continue the same program for another seven-day cycle or you may opt to create a new program.

## Making New Programs

You can create and make use of new programs using the formula from this chapter to accommodate goals for different target areas. It is recommended, however, that you only implement one seven-day program at a time. This is so your mind will stay focused on a single area for improvement and development. So, for instance, if you have aspirations to improve your physical health as well as your finances, it is recommended that you create, use, and finish a seven-day program for physical health before creating and employing one for career and finances.

# 6

## Compendium of Activities—The Power and Purpose of Everyday Tasks

This chapter serves as a reference for activities that may be used for your Self-Hypnosis Revolution programs. It first contains a list of activities you may choose from if you are creating your own program. The remainder of the chapter is a compendium that explains the symbolism of the activities and offers self-suggestions.

### How to Use This Chapter

If you are using a ready-to-go program, as found in Chapter 4 or in Appendix A, look up each of the listed activities in the Compendium. Read the key associations and explanations offered so you understand the symbolic significance of each activity.

If you are creating a custom program, select up to six activities from the Activity List on the next page. Then look up each activity you've chosen in the Compendium. Study the activity's key associations and explanation and choose one self-suggestion from those offered that corresponds to your target area. Transfer the key associations and the self-suggestions you select to your planning template.

### How Listings Are Arranged

The activities in the Compendium are arranged in alphabetical order. Each listing includes the name of the activity, beneath which the key associations are enumerated. Then self-suggestions are offered for each of the five possible target areas of development. Where "n/a" appears, no self-suggestion is offered for the target area because the metaphor doesn't adequately relate to that area of development.

## Activity List

Applying Makeup (general)
Applying Makeup: Foundation
Applying Makeup: Lipstick
Applying Makeup: Rouge
Arising
Arriving
Awakening
Baby Care (general)
Baby Care: Diapering
Baby Care: Feeding
Baking
Bathing (general)
Bathing: Bath
Bathing: Shower
Breathing
Brushing Teeth
Buying
Car Maintenance (general)
Car Maintenance: Brake
    Repair/Maintenance
Car Maintenance:
    Changing/Adding Oil
Car Maintenance: Maintaining,
    Changing, and Inflating Tires
Changing a Light Bulb
Changing Linens
Chewing
Childcare
Cleaning (general)
Cleaning: Basement
Cleaning: Bathroom
Cleaning: Bedroom
Cleaning: Closets
Cleaning: Clothes

Cleaning: Dishes
Cleaning: Floors
Cleaning: Kitchen
Cleaning: Living Room
Cleaning: Windows
Climbing Stairs
Communicating (general)
Communicating: Cell Phone
Communicating: Mail/Email
Communicating: Telephone
Computer Tasks
Cooking (general)
Cooking: Adding Spices
Cooking: Dessert
Cooking: Meat
Cooking: Pasta
Cooking: Vegetables
Crossing a Street
Descending Stairs
Dressing
Drinking (general)
Drinking: Coffee/Tea
Drinking: Juice
Drinking: Milk
Drinking: Water
Drinking: Wine
Driving (general)
Driving: Children
Driving: Home
Driving: School
Driving: Store
Driving: Work
Eating (general)
Eating: Fruit
Eating: Meat
Eating: Vegetables
Entering a Doorway

Exercising
Exiting
Fueling a Car
Gardening (general)
Gardening: Fertilizing
Gardening: Planting Seeds
Gardening: Tilling Soil
Gardening: Watering
Gardening: Weeding
Getting the Mail
Grooming
Home Improvement
Ironing Clothes
Knitting
Lawn Mowing
Listening
Office Chores
Paying Bills
Pet Care (general)
Pet Care: Birds
Pet Care: Cats
Pet Care: Dogs
Pet Care: Fish
Pet Care: Horses
Pet Care: Mice (Rodents)
Pet Care: Rabbits
Pet Care: Snakes
Plugging in an Appliance
Polishing (general)
Polishing: Floors
Polishing: Gold
Polishing: Shoes
Polishing: Silver
Polishing: Wood
Pouring Liquid
Recycling
Riding in an Elevator

Schoolwork
Sewing
Sexual Activity
Shopping
Sitting
Sleeping
Sports and Games (general)
Sports and Games: Archery
Sports and Games: Baseball
Sports and Games: Basketball
Sports and Games: Bicycling
Sports and Games: Boating/Sailing
Sports and Games: Cards
Sports and Games: Checkers/Chess
Sports and Games: Dancing
Sports and Games: Fishing
Sports and Games: Football
Sports and Games: Gambling
Sports and Games: Golf
Sports and Games: Jump Rope
Sports and Games: *Monopoly*
Sports and Games: Puzzles
Sports and Games: Running
Sports and Games: Skating
Sports and Games: Skiing
Sports and Games: Soccer
Sports and Games: Swimming
Sports and Games: Tennis
Sports and Games: Trivia
Sports and Games: Video Games
Sports and Games: Working Out
Sports and Games: Wrestling
Standing Up
Starting the Car
Taking out the Trash

Touching
Traveling
Turning on a Light
Tying Your Shoes
Unlocking a Door
Unplugging
Using the Toilet
Vacuuming
Waiting
Walking
Washing Hands
Watching
Working (general)
Working: Accountant
Working: Actor
Working: Administrative
  Assistant
Working: Agent
Working: Architect
Working: Athlete
Working: Automotive Mechanic
Working: Banker
Working: Broadcaster
Working: Business Developer
Working: Computer Programmer
Working: Construction Worker
Working: Consultant
Working: Customer Service
Working: Designer
Working: Distribution/Shipping
Working: Educator
Working: Engineer
Working: Entertainer
Working: Executive
Working: Fire and Rescue
Working: General Labor
Working: Government Worker

Working: Health Care Provider
Working: Hotel/Hospitality
  Worker
Working: Human Resources
Working:
  Installation/Maintenance/
  Repair
Working: Insurance
  Agent/Worker
Working: Inventory
Working: Law Enforcer
Working: Legal/Lawyer
Working: Mail Carrier
Working: Management
Working: Manufacturer
Working: Marketer
Working: Nurse
Working: Pharmaceutical Worker
Working: Professional Services
Working: Publisher
Working: Quality Control
Working: Researcher
Working: Restaurant/Food
  Service Worker
Working: Salesperson
Working: Telecommunications
Working: Therapist
Working: Trainer
Working: Transportation
Working: Warehouse Worker

Activities

## Compendium

**Applying Makeup (general)**

Key Associations: self-enhancement, positivism, self-image

Applying makeup is a way of enhancing aspects of one's appearance while downplaying perceived flaws. Metaphorically, this activity is about all aspects of self-enhancement and accentuating what is beautiful and positive about the self. It's interesting and appropriate to this metaphor that application is usually performed in front of a mirror, for a mirror represents self-image and identity. You could say that the makeup ritual is symbolic for affirming a more beautiful identity. As you apply makeup, realize this activity is anything but superficial, as some espouse. Begin to recognize that how you present and identify yourself to yourself is what is most important.

**Physical Wellness**

*"I identify myself as healthy and full of vitality."*

*"I accentuate and identify myself with beauty."*

**Mental Wellness**

*"I accentuate the beautiful aspects of my mind and personality "*

*"I identify and bring out all that is positive within me."*

**Career and Finances**

*n/a*

**Relationships**

*"I bring forward the positive and beautiful from within so I may enjoy the best relationships."*

**Spirituality**

*"I identify with the beautiful aspects of my soul."*

Activities

## Applying Makeup: Foundation
### Key Associations: core self-image, foundational enhancement

Foundation is a base or primary coating upon which other "colors" are added. Applying foundation is symbolic for creating or enhancing your own self-image at its very core—its foundation.

**Physical Wellness**

*"I create a foundation of physical beauty and health."*

**Mental Wellness**

*"I express to myself a foundation of beautiful, positive thoughts and feelings."*

**Career and Finances**

*n/a*

**Relationships**

*"I beautify the foundation of my relationships."*

**Spirituality**

*"I lay a beautiful spiritual foundation for my life."*

## Applying Makeup: Lipstick
### Key Associations: feminine self-image or enhancement

Lipstick highlights what is commonly considered one of the most feminine or sensual body parts. Applying lipstick, therefore, can be a metaphor for expressing, affirming, and enhancing all aspects of femininity.

**Physical Wellness**

*"I develop and express my feminine physical form."*

**Mental Wellness**

*"I identify and express my femininity."*

**Career and Finances**

*"I affirm and use my feminine powers in my career."*

**Relationships**

*"I see and express my sensuality in my romantic relationships."*

**Spirituality**

*"I celebrate my feminine sensuality as a reflection and expression of the divine."*

68

## Applying Makeup: Rouge
### Key Associations: healthy enhancement or self-image

Rouge creates a look of robust health on the cheeks. It's a symbol for enhancing or presenting that which is healthy and vital.

**Physical Wellness**
*"I create and express a healthy body image."*

**Mental Wellness**
*"I see myself as a healthy and vital personality."*

**Career and Finances**
*"I add vitality to my career and finances."*

**Relationships**
*"I express health and vitality in my relationships."*

**Spirituality**
*"I recognize and express a healthy, robust spirit."*

Activities

# Arising
## Key Associations: action, volition

Arising, whether from sleep or just getting up from a seated or prone position, carries with it the inner idea of taking action in the meeting of one's personal challenges. It's one thing to awaken to the reality of a given situation; it's another to "rise to the occasion" of dealing with it. To get up implies the notion of taking responsibility for one's affairs in a proactive manner.

**Physical Wellness**

*"I rise up and take responsibility for my physical health."*
*"I rise to meet health challenges and take action toward total recovery."*

**Mental Wellness**

*"I take action in order to establish and maintain healthy thinking patterns."*

**Career and Finances**

*"I rise to the challenges in my career."*
*"I get up and take action to create success and abundance for myself."*
*"I arise to better ways of handling my finances."*

**Relationships**

*"I get up and actively take part in fostering beneficial relationships."*
*"I arise to greet the dawning of renewed love in my life."*

**Spirituality**

*"I rise up and take active steps on my spiritual path."*
*"I arise to the call of the divine."*
*"I joyfully rise to meet the spiritual challenges this day may hold."*

---

## Arriving

### Key Associations: manifestation, achievement

It is common in English to hear "someone's arrived," used as a metaphor for noting career or financial achievement. But the metaphor needn't be limited to career and finances; it can be used to encourage the positive manifestation of any goal or state of improvement. As you arrive at different destinations, realize that your effort toward self-improvement can and will have a definite result.

**Physical Wellness**

*"I arrive at my destination of physical health."*

*"I arrive at my destination of physical fitness and attractiveness."*

**Mental Wellness**

*"I arrive at a balanced state of mind."*

*"I arrive at clear thinking and restored memory."*

**Career and Finances**

*"I arrive at my destination of success and abundance."*

**Relationships**

*"I arrive at my goal to have healthy and beneficial relationships."*

**Spirituality**

*"I arrive in my spiritual aspirations."*

*"I arrive in a beautiful understanding of the divine."*

## Awakening
### Key Associations: realization, recognition

The symbolic meaning of awakening from sleep, whether in the morning or some other time, deals with recognition or realization. I remember a rather blunt boss of mine once telling me to "wake up and smell the coffee," a saying you probably know. She meant that I should recognize some perceived truth or concept I'd missed, to clear away misunderstanding and see the reality of the situation. As you awaken from sleep, recognize your ability to realize accurately what is happening as the first step to changing it.

**Physical Wellness**

*"I awaken to opportunities to improve my body and health."*

**Mental Wellness**

*"I realize perfect balance in my thoughts and emotions."*

**Career and Finances**

*"I awaken to greater opportunities for success and abundance."*

*"I wake up to realize the material abundance that is manifesting for me."*

*"I open my eyes this day to what I can do to achieve my goals."*

**Relationships**

*"I awaken to a loving disposition in my relationships."*

*"I recognize the support and friendship that awaits me this day."*

*"I realize my ability to receive and give more love."*

**Spirituality**

*"I awaken now to greater realization of myself and truth."*

*"I open my eyes to recognize the principles of the divine in my life."*

*"I awaken to the love and presence of the divine in my life."*

Activities

## Baby Care (general)
### Key Associations: self-love, self-trust

Within each of us there always remains a part that is infant-like, needing love, nurturing, and a sense of security. Taking care of a baby is symbolic of totally and unconditionally loving ourselves and learning to trust the inner parent or guardian. As you take care of a baby, consider how you can be more loving to yourself. Recognize that what you say to yourself isn't nearly as important as the tone when you say it. Think of how you are building more self-trust as you take care of yourself.

**Physical Wellness**
*"I support the most basic needs of my body so it can grow strong and safe."*

**Mental Wellness**
*"I love and support the infant within so I feel protected and nourished."*

**Career and Finances**
*"I love and support my new ideas for success."*

**Relationships**
*"I love and protect myself in any relationship."*

**Spirituality**
*"The divine spirit unconditionally loves, protects, and supports me."*

## Baby Care: Diapering
### Key Associations: changing immature attitudes

Changing diapers is symbolic for needing to change or throw out immature or "babyish" ways or attitudes. While it is natural to nurture our inner infant, part of that involves cleaning up the messes we naturally create.

**Physical Wellness**

*"I change my immature attitudes and actions regarding my body."*

**Mental Wellness**

*"I change immature ways of thinking and doing."*

**Career and Finances**

*"I change my immature attitudes toward money and career choices."*

**Relationship**

*"I change my immature behaviors and attitudes in my relationships."*

**Spirituality**

*"I change and discard immature beliefs that no longer serve me."*

## Baby Care: Feeding
### Key Associations: self-nurturance

Feeding a baby is a metaphor for nurturing the most vulnerable parts of the self. This may apply, for example, to one's body image or to some fledgling idea for some area of life.

**Physical Wellness**

*"I take tender care of my physical body and give it what it needs to grow stronger."*

**Mental Wellness**

*"I lovingly feed my mind with gentle thoughts to help it become stronger."*

**Career and Finances**

*"I nurture my ideas for a better career and growing finances."*

**Relationships**

*"I nurture my new relationships so they can grow to maturity."*

**Spirituality**

*"I nurture my soul with loving beliefs about myself and the divine."*

## Baking
### Key Associations: creating, formulating

Because measurement is so important in baking, this activity is a metaphor for the time, careful formulations, and measurements that must be taken to improve the self in any area. Details are important in life just as they are in baking—if you want a good result. As you go about the process of baking, consider how being precise in your target areas may help you manifest the improvement you desire. Also consider that waiting until it's done is part of the process. You don't want to be "half-baked."

**Physical Wellness**
*"I take careful measures to create a healthy, attractive body."*

**Mental Wellness**
*"I take specific actions and careful measures to create clear and productive thoughts."*

**Career and Finances**
*"I recognize and take measured steps to create a strong financial future."*
*"I recognize and take precise steps to create a strong career."*

**Relationships**
*"I carefully establish good relationships and let them rise to maturity."*

**Spirituality**
*"The divine perfectly directs and measures my steps to make me a new creation."*

# Bathing (general)
## Key Associations: purification, release

The deeper meaning behind the activity of bathing deals with purification—letting go of what is unwanted or no longer of use so only health and purity remain. Note that purification needn't be seen from a puritanical or particularly moralistic perspective. To purify something is to return it to its true condition, its actual self—to remove contaminants or accumulated debris.

**Physical Wellness**

*"I wash away all sickness and disease from my mind and body."*
*"I purify myself from all undesirable conditions and am perfectly healthy."*

**Mental Wellness**

*"I slough away impurities of mind and body to become completely well."*
*"I slough off old patterns of thought to make room for the new."*
*"I cleanse myself of all accumulated anger, resentment, fear, and self-doubt."*

**Career and Finances**

*"I release all ideas and feelings that keep me from succeeding."*

**Relationships**

*"I wash away negative feelings about those I care about."*

**Spirituality**

*"I purify myself from all negative vibrations."*
*"I cleanse my inner self to let my inner light shine brighter."*
*"I wash away all impurities of mind and soul."*

## Bathing: Bath
### Key Associations: deep purification

Because of the total immersion in a bathtub and the penetrating heat of the water, taking a bath is a symbol for the deep purification of self. It's a metaphor for release that goes beneath conscious awareness.

**Physical Wellness**

*"I deeply purify and release my body from all sickness and disease."*
*"I allow deep healing to take place within my body."*

**Mental Wellness**

*"I deeply release all unhealthy conditions of mind and thought."*

**Career and Finances**

*"I deeply purify myself of hidden fears and limiting beliefs about success."*

**Relationships**

*"I deeply purify myself from limiting attitudes about relationships."*

**Spirituality**

*"I immerse myself in divine love that purifies and heals my soul."*

Activities

## Bathing: Shower
### Key Associations: release, drainage

Showering not only represents release but, because of the active drainage of dirty water, also symbolically emphasizes negativity and unwanted conditions being actively taken away.

**Physical Wellness**

*"I release all sickness from my body and send it down the drain."*

**Mental Wellness**

*"I let all unusable thoughts and feelings go down the drain."*

**Career and Finances**

*"I release all self-limiting beliefs about success down the drain."*

**Relationships**

*"I let all harmful beliefs in my relationships go down the drain."*

**Spirituality**

*"I send all undesirable vibrations down the drain for recycling."*
*"I release self-limiting patterns down the drain."*

## Breathing
### Key Associations: assimilation, release, life

Breathing is a sign and symbol of life itself. The intake of breath is the assimilation of air, which represents taking in the essence of life and spirit. Exhalation represents relaxation and release of that which we cannot use. As you breathe in, realize you are drawing into your orbit that which you need to live and thrive. When you exhale, recognize that letting go of that which is no longer useful is very important for life to continue.

### Physical Wellness

*"I draw life and energy into my body."*

*"I oxygenate my body and release what I can no longer use."*

### Mental Wellness

*"I draw in positive thoughts and relax my emotions."*

*"I give my thoughts and feelings plenty of room to breathe."*

### Career and Finances

*"I breathe life into my career and finances."*

*"I draw in what I can use in my business, and release what is no longer helpful."*

### Relationships

*"I breathe fresh air into my relationships."*

*"I draw fresh, healthy relationships to me and release those that must move on."*

### Spirituality

*"The divine breathes life into me at every moment of my life."*

Activities

## Brushing Teeth
### Key Associations: maintaining power

Teeth are a symbol for independence and power. We brush our teeth to keep them strong and healthy. This is a symbolic act for purifying or maintaining a sense of power and independence. As you brush your teeth, recognize your ability and responsibility to keep your focus on improvement consistent and steadfast.

**Physical Wellness**

*"I recognize and maintain my physical powers."*

**Mental Wellness**

*"I purify my mind of fragmented thoughts to keep it strong and powerful."*

**Career and Finances**

*"I focus on the healthy maintenance of my career and finances."*

**Relationships**

*"I recognize my power to keep my relationships strong and healthy."*

**Spirituality**

*"I purify and maintain my spiritual aspirations."*
*"I purify and maintain my spiritual power."*

## Buying
### Key Associations: acceptance, investing

Buying or purchasing items can be understood as a metaphor for accepting or investing uplifting beliefs about the self and circumstances. This correspondence with acceptance or lack thereof is noted in colloquialisms such as "I'll buy that" or "I don't buy it." When purchasing an item of any kind, consider "buying into" thoughts and ideas to improve in your target areas. Note that buying and shopping are not identical in their symbolic meanings.

**Physical Wellness**
*"I buy into the idea of having and maintaining a healthy body."*
*"I buy into the belief that my body is beautiful."*

**Mental Wellness**
*"I buy into the notion of a centered state of mind."*

**Career and Finances**
*"I invest myself in a very successful career."*
*"I buy into the principle that abundant finances are good for me."*

**Relationships**
*"I buy into healthy relationships."*

**Spirituality**
*"I buy into my belief in the divine."*
*"I invest in my spiritual principles."*
*"I buy into the idea that the divine loves and cares for me."*

## Car Maintenance (general)
### Key Associations: self-preservation, power

Your car is a symbol for your ego, your personality, or even your body. To perform any sort of car maintenance is symbolic of the upkeep or preservation of your sense of self and your sense of control over your life. A car can also represent your physical body. As you perform car maintenance or when you take the car to the mechanic, consider the importance of maintaining your sense of who you are in the world. Recognize your ability to exert power and influence over your environment and what you can do to keep it intact.

**Physical Wellness**
*"I regularly maintain my body to function perfectly and efficiently."*

**Mental Wellness**
*"I preserve my sense of self and recognize my personal power."*

**Career and Finances**
*n/a*

**Relationships**
*"I maintain my sense of self and personal power amidst my relationships."*

**Spirituality**
*"I maintain and identify myself as a powerful vehicle of the divine."*

Activities

## Car Maintenance: Brake Repair/Maintenance
### Key Associations: self-control

Repairing or maintaining the brakes on a vehicle is a symbol for the restoration or maintenance of our self-control over the vehicle of personality. Knowing when to slow down or stop ourselves from certain attitudes and behaviors is just as important as knowing when to "step on the gas."

**Physical Wellness**

*"I put the brakes on beliefs and behaviors that might harm my body."*

**Mental Wellness**

*"I restore and maintain control over what I think about myself."*
*"I put the brakes on potentially destructive thoughts and mental habits."*

**Career and Finances**

*"I maintain control over my identity in relationship to success and money."*

**Relationships**

*"I maintain self-control amidst all of my relationships."*

**Spirituality**

*"I gain self-control so I may enjoy a spiritual identity."*

## Car Maintenance: Changing/Adding Oil
### Key Associations: self-change, renewal

Oil is added or changed in a vehicle to keep the engine lubricated and running. This is a wonderful metaphor for the adding or changing of beliefs, attitudes, and behaviors so our lives function efficiently. Without this regular change, like an engine, we run the risk of "freezing up."

**Physical Wellness**
*"I add and change healthy choices to maintain the proper functions of my body."*

**Mental Wellness**
*"I add and change my attitudes and beliefs about myself to be happier and productive."*

**Career and Finances**
*"I add and change my ideas about my abilities to be successful."*

**Relationships**
*"I renew my attitudes about myself in my relationships."*

**Spirituality**
*"I renew my beliefs and attitudes about myself in relation to the divine."*

## Car Maintenance: Maintaining, Changing, and Inflating Tires
### Key Associations: self-support

Tires are what support a vehicle so it can reach its destination. Changing or inflating tires is a metaphor for giving self-support to the ego, to affirming who we are to ourselves.

**Physical Wellness**

*"I support myself in having and maintaining a healthy, attractive body."*

**Mental Wellness**

*"I support my identity as a well-balanced individual of great value and merit."*

**Career and Finances**

*"I support my identity as a successful individual."*

**Relationships**

*"I support a strong sense of self and power in all of my relationships."*

**Spirituality**

*"I support my identity as a spiritual and profound individual."*

Activities

## Changing a Light Bulb
### Key Associations: new ideas, understanding

When we change a light bulb, we remove that which no longer serves its original function of illumination and replace it with that which does. This activity is symbolic for first removing "burnt out" ideas, behaviors, and patterns that once served a useful purpose but no longer function, and replacing them with new ones that provide knowledge and understanding. When changing a light bulb, realize whether there are many patterns of thought and behavior that no longer help you. Consider what options might provide more "light" in your life.

**Physical Wellness**

*"I remove from my life that which does not serve my body in exchange for that which does."*

**Mental Wellness**

*"I remove old thought patterns that no longer serve me for bright new ones that provide self-knowledge and understanding."*

**Career and Finances**

*"I replace burned-out ideas and aspirations about money and success with fresh knowledge and creativity that take me further."*

**Relationships**

*"I replace my burned-out attitudes and behaviors in my relationships with new ones to provide mutual insight and understanding."*

**Spirituality**

*"I replace burned-out ideas about the divine that no longer assist me for those that provide fresh illumination."*

## Changing Linens
### Key Associations: changing/purifying beliefs

The bed is (among other things) a symbol for foundations. Linens, which act as a covering, are a symbol for protection. Changing bed linens is a metaphor for the changing or purification of self-protective beliefs. And just as linens need to be changed and washed, our beliefs need to be changed and purified if they are to be of value to us. When changing linens, consider the value of modifying the beliefs you hold to create a more restful foundation for your life.

**Physical Wellness**

*"I change and purify my beliefs about my body, my health, and physical beauty."*

**Mental Wellness**

*"I change and purify self-protective beliefs to keep my mind healthy and peaceful."*

**Career and Finances**

*"I change and purify self-protective beliefs about success and money."*

**Relationships**

*"I change and purify self-protective beliefs about my relationships."*

**Spirituality**

*"I change and purify self-protective beliefs to find greater joy and comfort in the divine."*

88

## Chewing
### Key Associations: contemplation, consideration

Chewing is a common metaphor for giving detailed consideration to ideas or plans. Sayings like "let me chew on that" illustrate this perfectly. When chewing on food or gum, recognize your need to analyze and "mull over" your target areas. Realize that you will come to a resolution for positive change.

**Physical Wellness**

*"I chew on the prospect of having a healthy, fit, and attractive body."*

**Mental Wellness**

*"I chew on thoughts that help me feel at peace and happy with myself."*

**Career and Finances**

*"I chew on new ideas to bring me success and large sums of money."*

**Relationships**

*"I chew on the reality of having and maintaining loving, mutually beneficial relationships."*

**Spirituality**

*"I chew on the vision of a stronger connection with the divine."*

Activities

## Childcare
### Key Associations: self-development

Taking care of children is a symbolic activity for developing parts of self that are incomplete or immature. Generally, taking care of boys is symbolic for developing the active conscious self, while taking care of girls is symbolic for developing the inner and receptive aspects. The manner and attitude in which you take care of children is symbolic for how you treat these parts of yourself. So as you take care of and discipline your children, consider how you are simultaneously raising a part of yourself to maturity on a deep level.

**Physical Wellness**
*"I recognize my body's power and help it develop more strongly."*

**Mental Wellness**
*"My thoughts are like children, and I raise them to be positive and wise."*

**Career and Finances**
*"I lovingly parent my abilities and ideas to become more successful."*

**Relationships**
*"I help my relationships to grow strong and mature."*

**Spirituality**
*"My divine parent cares for and guides my soul to maturity."*

## Cleaning (general)
### Key Associations: purification, order, maintenance

Any type of cleaning, whether it's mopping, dusting, vacuuming, or straightening up is a metaphor for setting an aspect of life in order. Just as we must maintain our homes in order to have a sanitary and sensible environment, we must also purify our thoughts, put our finances in order, and maintain our relationships with others and with the divine so our lives and our inner environment continue to function properly. Cleaning can also be used to encourage purification of the body, its systems and functions.

**Physical Wellness**
*"I purify and maintain my body to be in perfect working order."*

**Mental Wellness**
*"I place my thoughts in proper and beautiful order."*
*"I clean my thoughts of accumulated confusion and I restore order."*

**Career and Finances**
*"I put my career and finances in proper working order."*
*"I organize and maintain my finances."*

**Relationships**
*"I maintain and prioritize my relationships."*

**Spirituality**
*"I purify and restore the beauty of my spiritual life."*
*"I maintain a healthy and orderly spiritual environment."*

## Cleaning: Basement
### Key Associations: subconscious and memory purification

The basement is a symbol for the part of the self that is beneath the surface of our awareness: the subconscious. Cleaning the basement may be used as an unparalleled activity for purging, purifying, and reordering systems of mind and body to be of assistance to conscious desires. This may include old hurts and memories. There is even great symbolism to be gleaned from things found in a basement, such as the heating unit or storage areas.

**Physical Wellness**

*"I purify and place in order all bodily systems to support perfect health."*

**Mental Wellness**

*"I purify and organize my deepest thoughts to establish a healthy, peaceful mind."*

**Career and Finances**

*"I purify and organize my subconscious beliefs to support success and abundance."*

**Relationships**

*"I clean my subconscious thoughts to establish and maintain good relationships."*

**Spirituality**

*"I clean and organize the deepest aspects of my soul to line up with my spiritual principles."*

## Cleaning: Bathroom
### Key Associations: purification maintenance

Cleaning the bathroom or any part of it is metaphorical for purifying or maintaining any tools used to purify body and mind. Cleaning the toilet, for instance, could suggest to the mind to keep the colon and urinary tract clear, as they are the tools we use to release waste. Many symbolic inferences may apply.

**Physical Wellness**

*"I purify my body's tools for elimination."*

**Mental Wellness**

*"I purify my mind's tools for elimination."*

**Career and Finances**

*n/a*

**Relationships**

*n/a*

**Spirituality**

*"I purify my soul's tools for elimination."*

Activities

## Cleaning: Bedroom
### Key Associations: intimacy, privacy, rest

The bedroom is a place of privacy, rest, and intimacy. Cleaning it is, therefore, symbolic for maintaining those aspects of our selves and our lives.

**Physical Wellness**

*"I maintain that which helps my body rest and restore itself."*

**Mental Wellness**

*"I maintain love and intimacy with my most private self."*

**Career and Finances**

*n/a*

**Relationships**

*"I maintain intimacy in my closest relationships."*

**Spirituality**

*"I maintain my space of spiritual rest and intimacy within me."*

## Cleaning: Closets
### Key Associations: releasing memories

Cleaning a closet is a symbol for clearing out hidden memories or negative feelings about the past.

**Physical Wellness**

*"I let go of past pains and secrets that keep me from enjoying perfect health."*

**Mental Wellness**

*"I clear away that which is past to make room for new thoughts and experiences."*

**Career and Finances**

*"I release memories and secret pains that keep me from achieving success."*

**Relationships**

*"I let go of past hurts I've stored to make room for love in my relationships."*

**Spirituality**

*"The divine helps me clear out hurtful and guilty memories to purify my soul."*

Activities

## Cleaning: Clothes
### Key Associations: self-image

Cleaning your clothes is symbolic for purifying or maintaining your sense of identity.

**Physical Wellness**

*"I purify and maintain my identity as a healthy, physical being."*

**Mental Wellness**

*"I purify and maintain my identity as a stable, vital, and healthy personality."*

**Career and Finances**

*"I purify and maintain my identity as a successful individual."*

**Relationships**

*"I purify and maintain my sense of self amidst all of my relationships."*

**Spirituality**

*"I purify and maintain my spiritual identity."*

## Cleaning: Dishes
### Key Associations: purification, nourishment

Washing dishes is a metaphor for purifying and maintaining that in our lives which is a vessel for our nourishment. This purification may be a completely psychological one. For instance, we might purify our attitudes about our job, for it is the vessel by which we receive monetary nourishment. Or we might need to adjust how we view our mate, who is a vessel for our emotional support.

**Physical Wellness**
*"I purify my body to be a fit and attractive vessel for me."*

**Mental Wellness**
*"I purify my thoughts so they can hold positive emotions."*

**Career and Finances**
*"I maintain my financial accounts so they contain my money successfully."*
*"I purify my thoughts about my job so it continues to provide what I need."*

**Relationships**
*"I purify my thoughts and attitudes about my relationships, so that they may continue to provide me with happiness and fulfillment."*

**Spirituality**
*"I purify my body and mind to be fit vessels for divine expression."*

Activities

## Cleaning: Floors
### Key Associations: belief purification, understanding

Because we stand on a floor, it is a symbol for understanding our most fundamental beliefs. As you clean the floor, recognize that your understanding of your life and circumstances is based on accepted beliefs. Consider what thoughts have "soiled" those beliefs or whether an adjustment to existing beliefs might be in order to achieve wanted change.

**Physical Wellness**

*"I cleanse myself of sullied beliefs about my body to restore perfect health."*
*"I purify my foundational beliefs about physical beauty."*

**Mental Wellness**

*"I cleanse troubling thoughts to restore the pure foundation of my mind."*

**Career and Finances**

*"I restore optimistic beliefs about my career and financial future."*

**Relationships**

*"I purify and maintain a loving foundation in my relationships."*

**Spirituality**

*"I purify my spiritual foundation and beliefs."*

## Cleaning: Kitchen
### Key Associations: productivity maintenance

The kitchen is a place where nourishment is prepared (and consumed) and cleaning it is a symbol for maintaining that which helps us to be productive in areas of our lives. On the physical level, the kitchen may refer to the stomach or small intestine, where nourishment is extracted. It can also represent productivity in our career and finances.

**Physical Wellness**

*"I purify and maintain my body's tools and organs for processing nourishment."*

**Mental Wellness**

*"I purify and maintain my mind's resources for processing thoughts and emotions."*

**Career and Finances**

*"I purify and maintain my productivity in my career and finances."*

**Relationships**

*"I purify and maintain my nourishing relationships."*

**Spirituality**

*"I purify and maintain my resources for spiritual nourishment."*

## Cleaning: Living Room
### Key Associations: central self-purification

The living room of a home is the center of much activity. Cleaning your living room is, therefore, a symbol for purifying and maintaining what is most central and important to the self.

**Physical Wellness**

*"I clean and maintain the body in which I reside."*

**Mental Wellness**

*"I clean and restore my most central self."*

**Career and Finances**

*"I clean up wasteful spending and use money for central needs."*

**Relationships**

*"I purify my core relationships and restore what is important."*

**Spirituality**

*"I purify my life and maintain my spiritual center."*

## Cleaning: Windows
### Key Associations: insight, restoration

We use windows to see outside or inside. They are the eyes of a house, and sight is a metaphor for recognition and observation. So cleaning a window is a symbol for removing that which obstructs the ability to recognize and observe truth about ourselves and circumstances. When washing a window, contemplate what's been in the way of seeing yourself and the situation accurately—and how you can remove it.

**Physical Wellness**

*"I remove all that obscures my vision of perfect health and attractiveness."*

**Mental Wellness**

*"I remove what obscures understanding of me and my life."*

**Career and Finances**

*"I remove what taints my vision of a bright and successful career."*

**Relationships**

*"I get rid of that which makes my relationships unclear."*

**Spirituality**

*"I remove that which obscures my vision of divine light."*

# Climbing Stairs
## Key Associations: effort, achievement

Just as we must use effort and muscles to climb stairs or a ladder, we often have goals that require effort to achieve. Climbing stairs (or a ladder) is a moving symbol for making strides to fulfill desires. The individual stairs or rungs remind us that we do not leap to the top, but that increments of effort are often required before we "reach the top." The principle in this metaphor may be poignantly applied to any life goals or any act of self-improvement. Climbing stairs requires strength and also builds strength in the climber—in contrast to a mechanical form of ascent, such as an escalator, in which the power is provided from an outside source. As you climb any flight of stairs (or a ladder), realize that most of your accomplishments and plans for self-improvement are the result of making an effort and taking specific action.

### Physical Wellness
*"I make my way, step by step, toward the pinnacle of health."*
*"I use my effort and climb closer and closer to total fitness."*

### Mental Wellness
*"I climb to the top of mental wellness and balance."*
*"I make my way, step by step, to the perfect expression of my personality."*

### Career and Finances
*"I use my effort to climb to the top of my profession."*
*"I work my way to the pinnacle of success."*
*"Step by step, I make my way to the top of financial success."*
*"I recognize the steps required to reach my goals."*

### Relationships
*"I recognize the steps I need to take toward the best relationships."*

### Spirituality
*"I take the steps required to reach the spiritual heights."*
*"I ascend toward divine understanding one step at a time."*

## Communicating (general)
### Key Associations: understanding, information, rapport

Communicating, in whatever form and by whatever medium, is associated with our ability to give and receive information, and includes issues of understanding, rapport, and accuracy in relaying thoughts and ideas, whether to ourselves or to others. We may use the task of communicating with those around us to enhance our ability to communicate with others, or as a means to establish better self-communication. As you communicate, whether in person, by phone, or by computer, recognize that you are in constant communication with yourself. Consider what messages you send yourself and how you might improve them.

**Physical Wellness**
*"I communicate health and vitality to my body, and I listen to the messages it sends me."*

**Mental Wellness**
*"I establish and maintain excellent rapport with all levels of my mind for balance and well-being."*

**Career and Finances**
*"I accurately communicate my ideas and intentions and receive due credit and compensation."*

**Relationships**
*"I accurately communicate with others and establish mutual understanding."*

**Spirituality**
*"I open communication to and from the divine."*

Activities

## Communicating: Cell Phone
### Key Associations: immediate rapport

Using a cell phone is symbolic for instant accessibility and rapport with aspects of self.

**Physical Wellness**

*"I access my body's ability to become healthy and strong."*

*"I have immediate rapport with my body to give and receive important messages."*

**Mental Wellness**

*"I have immediate rapport with my inner mind to develop self understanding."*

**Career and Finances**

*"I build immediate rapport with those who help me achieve my goals."*

**Relationships**

*"I establish immediate rapport to create understanding in new and existing relationships."*

**Spirituality**

*"I have immediate rapport with the divine."*

## Communicating: Mail/Email
### Key Associations: symbolic communication

Because mail and email use the written word, which is really a series of symbols, this is a metaphor for delivering messages, creating rapport, or developing understanding with others or the self through the use of symbols.

**Physical Wellness**

*"I deliver symbolic messages to my body to establish perfect health."*

**Mental Wellness**

*"I deliver symbolic messages of self-esteem and peace to my inner mind."*

**Career and Finances**

*"I deliver symbolic messages of success and wealth to my inner mind."*

**Relationships**

*"I deliver and receive symbolic messages to establish and maintain healthy relationships."*

**Spirituality**

*"I understand and utilize the language of love and spirit."*

## Communicating: Telephone
### Key Associations: seeking connection

A telephone provides a way to connect with someone at a distance. It's a metaphor for seeking or "reaching out" to others or to some aspect of self that might otherwise remain remote.

**Physical Wellness**

*"I reach out and communicate with my body to achieve total health."*

**Mental Wellness**

*"I seek self-understanding and communication with my inner mind."*

**Career and Finances**

*"I seek connection with those who can assist my success."*

**Relationships**

*"I reach out and connect with those I desire a relationship with."*

**Spirituality**

*"I reach out and connect with the divine voice."*

## Computer Tasks
### Key Associations: communication, programming

Computer activities contain many marvelous complex metaphors for communicating with ourselves and others, as well as understanding and changing our "programmed" behaviors and attitudes of mind and body. As you engage in computer-related tasks, recognize that your mind is like a computer—though infinitely more complex. Understand that you access and communicate with the programs of your mind every day, all day, and the quality of that interaction largely determines the quality of your life.

**Physical Wellness**

*"I communicate with and program my mind for perfect health."*

*"I now program my mind for a stronger, more beautiful body."*

**Mental Wellness**

*"I input clear and valuable thoughts and directives to my mind."*

**Career and Finances**

*"I program my mind to achieve successful outcomes in career and finances."*

**Relationships**

*"I communicate clearly and effectively with myself and others to attract and maintain good relationships."*

**Spirituality**

*"The divine interfaces with me and upgrades my spiritual programming."*

*"I communicate and program myself with strong spiritual principles and aspirations."*

## Cooking (general)
### Key Associations: preparation, creation, formulation

Cooking is an activity that includes preparation, formulation, and creation. There are familiar sayings like "cooking up a scheme" or "cooking up some new ideas" that highlight the metaphorical content of this task. It may be applied to any kind of plan; anything that requires a process or specific steps (as in a recipe) to produce a desired result. It is also notable that many people like to get creative as they cook and experiment with ingredients, suggesting that deviation from a formula can lead to self-discovery. As you cook, consider what you need to prepare in your target area in order to "taste" success.

**Physical Wellness**

"I prepare nutritious and delicious food for my body."

**Mental Wellness**

"I form marvelous patterns and combinations of thought."

"I process my thoughts to create joyful experiences."

**Career and Finances**

"I cook up new and excellent ways to make more money."

"I follow a recipe for success."

"I create a tasteful and comfortable lifestyle."

**Relationships**

"I have all the right ingredients to have wonderful relationships."

**Spirituality**

"My spiritual life is in process."

"I utilize the right ingredients to reach spiritual attainment."

Activities

## Cooking: Adding Spices
### Key Associations: self-stimulation, interest

Adding spices to your food as you cook is a metaphor for stimulating yourself with interesting and exciting experiences.

**Physical Wellness**

*"I add wonderful and interesting activities to make my body feel more alive."*

**Mental Wellness**

*"I add new and interesting sources of thought to keep my mind sharp and active."*

**Career and Finances**

*"I add spice to my career to make it more fun and interesting."*

**Relationships**

*"I incorporate new people and experiences into my life."*

**Spirituality**

*"I incorporate variety into my life to stimulate my spirit in uplifting directions."*

## Cooking: Dessert
### Key Associations: preparing pleasurable outcomes, reward

Because they are sweet, desserts are associated with experiencing pleasure. Cooking dessert is, therefore, a symbol for preparing for a pleasurable outcome or reward, as desserts are eaten at the end of a meal.

**Physical Wellness**

*"I prepare to receive the sweet reward of a healthy and appealing body."*

**Mental Wellness**

*"I prepare to enjoy the sweet reward of a healthy, balanced mind."*

**Career and Finances**

*"I prepare to enjoy the sweetness of success and abundant riches."*

**Relationships**

*"I prepare to enjoy the sweetness of love and intimacy in my relationships."*

**Spirituality**

*"I prepare to enjoy the sweet reward of divine love and peace."*

## Cooking: Meat
### Key Associations: preparing substantial sustenance

Cooking meat is representative of preparing that which will provide substantial sustenance to mind, body, and spirit. Meat can also represent complex principles or concepts.

**Physical Wellness**

*"I prepare to provide my body with what it needs to sustain itself."*

**Mental Wellness**

*"I prepare to provide my mind substantial knowledge to grow strong and wise."*

**Career and Finances**

*"I prepare to provide myself with substantial sources of income."*

**Relationships**

*"I prepare to provide myself with hearty and substantial relationships."*

**Spirituality**

*"I prepare to provide myself with deep and substantial spiritual knowledge for my soul to feast on."*

## Cooking: Pasta
### Key Associations: preparation for satisfaction, fulfillment

Cooking pasta is a metaphor for preparing that which provides fulfillment and satisfaction in our lives.

**Physical Wellness**

*"I prepare to provide my body with all it needs to be healthy and satisfied."*

**Mental Wellness**

*"I prepare to provide my mind with fulfilling and satisfying ideas and knowledge."*

**Career and Finances**

*"I prepare to provide myself with a satisfying and fulfilling career and lifestyle."*

**Relationships**

*"I prepare to provide myself with satisfaction and fulfillment in my relationships."*

**Spirituality**

*"I prepare to provide myself with satisfaction and fulfillment from spiritual sources."*

Activities

## Cooking: Vegetables
### Key Associations: preparation for health

Cooking vegetables is symbolic for preparing to assimilate into the self that is natural and health producing.

**Physical Wellness**

*"I prepare for my body that which it can use to produce optimum health."*

**Mental Wellness**

*"I prepare to assimilate thoughts and ideas that promote good mental health."*

**Career and Finances**

*"I prepare ideas and beliefs that produce a healthy career and finances."*

**Relationships**

*"I prepare to draw to myself that which produces healthy relationships."*

**Spirituality**

*"I prepare to assimilate principles and disciplines that create a healthy spirit."*

## Crossing a Street
### Key Associations: change, movement, transition

Crossing a street provides a metaphor related to movement or changes that require wisdom and courage. For just as we ought to use wisdom to look both ways before crossing any street, the possible ramifications of intended actions should be carefully considered before setting them in motion. This "look before you leap" notion can be applied to issues of body, mind, relationships, and of course career. It should also be noted we cross a street "to get to the other side," as the old chicken joke proclaims. Symbolically, this "other side" might be a better life, relationship, or financial situation. The act of crossing is representative of the transition of getting from one stage of development to the other. As you cross any street, realize that you have the ability to make changes and that you can handle the transitions with confidence.

**Physical Wellness**
*"I make changes to my body and diet with wisdom and discretion."*

**Mental Wellness**
*"I make the transition to a better frame of mind."*

**Career and Finances**
*"I take calculated financial risks in order to cross over to a better life."*
*"I cross over to a better career."*

**Relationships**
*"I take the risks necessary to have wonderful relationships."*

**Spirituality**
*"I cross over to the spiritual side of life."*

## Descending Stairs
### Key Associations: practicality, manifestation, deepening

Walking down steps is a symbol in motion for taking knowledge or growth and bringing it "down" to the practical world where it can have the most impact. This is a wonderful metaphor for taking our "lofty" ideas and finding the incremental "steps" to see them manifested in the real world. Descending stairs can also represent access to the deeper or subconscious levels of the mind. The idea of using effort and taking things step by step is also represented.

**Physical Wellness**
*"I take my knowledge of physical wellness into practical application."*

**Mental Wellness**
*"I access deep levels of thought and feeling to enhance my life."*

**Career and Finances**
*"I take my ideas and talents into the world."*
*"I bring my moneymaking ideas down to a practical level."*

**Relationships**
*"I access deeper levels in my close relationships."*

**Spirituality**
*"I take my spiritual insights down into my everyday life."*
*"I apply my spiritual insights into the realm of manifestation."*

## Dressing
### Key Associations: identity, self-image

The idea of getting dressed has symbolic associations with your sense of who you are to yourself and to others. For instance, if you are dressing to go to work, you put on clothes that identify you with the type of work you do, whether it's a suit, dress, uniform, or painter's pants. In a broader sense, every time we dress we have an opportunity to reestablish that we recognize who we are and the roles we play in life and to encourage the highest sense of self in our daily activities. Sometimes we even dress to affect our emotions. We can choose to "put on" a positive mood and may find our true emotions catching up with this ideal. As you get dressed, think about what part of your identity you want to affirm and assert.

**Physical Wellness**
*"I affirm my identity as a healthy, attractive individual."*

**Mental Wellness**
*"I identify myself as someone who is mentally healthy and powerful."*

**Career and Finances**
*"I dress for success, abundance, and opportunity to excel in my career."*
*"I identify myself as successful and allow others to see me that way."*
*"I am suited to prosperity and wealth."*

**Relationships**
*"I identify myself as a loving partner and friend."*
*"I play the authentic role of a passionate and generous individual."*

**Spirituality**
*"I express my individual spirit and enjoy my divine identity."*

Activities

## Drinking (general)
### Key Associations: satisfaction, spirituality, purification

We drink in order to quench the body's thirst. Liquid, in general, is associated with the emotions and with consciousness. Thus, drinking can be symbolic for seeking out and satisfying an inner thirst for that which makes you feel alive, happy, or excited. It can also be symbolic for quenching a thirst for spiritual truth of a direct experiential nature. "Drinking in" carries with it the idea of partaking of life experiences.

**Physical Wellness**

*"I quench and refresh the cells of my body for optimum health and performance."*

*"I purify my body of all toxins."*

**Mental Wellness**

*"I satisfy my need for experiences that make me feel healthy and alive."*

*"I purify myself of all toxic feelings."*

*"I quench my desire to feel and experience that which I need."*

**Career and Finances**

*"I drink in optimistic thoughts and feelings of success and prosperity."*

*"I imbibe the wealth and abundance of life in its fullness."*

*"I quench my thirst for success and material supply."*

**Relationships**

*"I drink in love and acceptance from those around me."*

*"I am quenched by the love I receive in my relationships."*

**Spirituality**

*"I quench my thirst for spiritual knowledge."*

*"I drink my fill from the divine source."*

*"I take in truth and purity of spirit."*

Activities

## Drinking: Coffee/Tea
### Key Associations: stimulation

Drinking coffee or tea is associated with stimulation or the evocation of uplifting emotions due to the caffeine often found in these liquids.

**Physical Wellness**

*"I stimulate my body into activities that promote optimal health."*

**Mental Wellness**

*"I stimulate my mind with emotions that make me feel alive and well."*

**Career and Finances**

*"I drink in stimulating and uplifting emotions about my career and finances."*

**Relationships**

*"I stimulate uplifting emotions about the people I care about."*

**Spirituality**

*"I am stimulated into spiritual passion and dedication."*

## Drinking: Juice
### Key Associations: pleasant emotions

Because fruit juice is sweet, drinking it is a symbol for experiencing "sweet" events and emotions.

**Physical Wellness**

*"I enjoy the sweetness of life that this body allows me to feel."*

**Mental Wellness**

*"I drink in that which lets me experience sweet feelings."*

**Career and Finances**

*n/a*

**Relationships**

*"I drink from the nectar of loving relationships."*

**Spirituality**

*"I drink in the sweetness of the divine spirit."*

## Drinking: Milk
### Key Associations: kindness, nurturance

Milk has many associations, among which are maternal love and kindness. So drinking milk is symbolic for providing the emotional sustenance of kindness to the self.

**Physical Wellness**

*"I nourish and nurture my body with kindness and good treatment."*

**Mental Wellness**

*"I nourish and nurture my mind with kind thoughts and attitudes."*

**Career and Finances**

*n/a*

**Relationships**

*n/a*

**Spirituality**

*"I nourish and nurture my soul with kindness and self-supporting beliefs."*

## Drinking: Water
### Key Associations: life, purification

Because the intake of water is essential to sustain life, drinking it is a symbol for the experience of living. It can carry a connotation of purification, as water is also used to clean. Water is a symbol for consciousness and emotion as well.

**Physical Wellness**

*"I purify my body with the water of life."*

**Mental Wellness**

*"I vitalize my emotions and drink in the essence of life."*

**Career and Finances**

*n/a*

**Relationships**

*n/a*

**Spirituality**

*"I drink from the pure water of divine consciousness."*

## Drinking: Wine
### Key Associations: pleasure, goodness

Drinking wine is a symbol for experiencing and savoring that which is pleasurable and good in life.

**Physical Wellness**
*"I drink in the pleasures of sensation that my body allows me to feel."*

**Mental Wellness**
*"I drink in the joy and goodness I experience in my life."*

**Career and Finances**
*"I drink in the pleasures of success and abundance."*

**Relationships**
*"I drink in the pleasures and goodness of my relationships."*

**Spirituality**
*"I drink in the joy and goodness of the divine."*

## Driving (general)
### Key Associations: motivation, passion, self-control

Driving involves guiding a powered vehicle toward some destination. On a deeper level, your passions and motivations "drive you" to create the life you want. The act of driving can be recognized as a symbolic activity for "steering" yourself into idealized forms of action, which then manifest your goals—whatever they may be. As you drive anywhere, recognize that all of your serious aspirations require determination and a clear idea of how to attain them.

**Physical Wellness**

*"I drive myself toward ever greater health and wellness."*

**Mental Wellness**

*"I drive myself toward clear thinking and emotional balance."*

**Career and Finances**

*"I have a strong drive to succeed in making money."*

*"I drive myself closer and closer to success."*

*"I am on the right road for my career aspirations."*

**Relationships**

*"I steer my relationships toward mutual trust and respect."*

**Spirituality**

*"I drive myself toward spirit and truth."*

*"My drive toward spiritual discipline is strong and vital."*

Activities

## Driving: Children
### Key Associations: cultivation of desire

Children can represent childlike or undeveloped aspects of self or unfinished projects. Driving children to some destination can represent a desire to assist those aspects or projects in order to help them mature. Note that where you drive children can also have inner significance.

**Physical Wellness**

*"I drive my changing body toward healthy and mature development."*

**Mental Wellness**

*"I drive my developing mind to areas of thought that assist health and maturity."*

**Career and Finances**

*"I drive my young projects and fresh ideas into successful maturity."*

**Relationships**

*"I drive my young relationships toward healthy maturity."*

**Spirituality**

*"I drive my youthful soul to experiences that promote healing and maturity."*

## Driving: Home
### Key Associations: self-knowledge

Home is a symbol for the self. Driving home, therefore, is symbolic for having the motivation for knowing yourself and all that is truly important to you.

**Physical Wellness**

*"I drive myself to understand my body and its importance to me."*

**Mental Wellness**

*"I drive myself to understand my thoughts, attitudes, and behaviors."*

**Career and Finances**

*"I drive myself to understanding what makes me feel successful."*

**Relationships**

*"I drive myself to understand how I think and behave with others."*

**Spirituality**

*"I drive to understand the nature of true spirit."*

# Driving: School
## Key Associations: passion for knowledge

Driving to school is a metaphor for having a passion for knowledge and understanding for self, for others, and for life.

**Physical Wellness**

*"I drive myself to knowledge that will make and keep my body healthy."*

**Mental Wellness**

*"I drive myself to the knowledge and understanding of my mind."*
*"I drive myself to greater knowledge and understanding of life."*

**Career and Finances**

*"I drive myself to knowledge that assists my abundant success."*

**Relationships**

*"I drive myself to understand my relationships better."*

**Spirituality**

*"I drive myself to knowledge of the divine."*

Activities

## Driving: Store
### Key Associations: passion for choice

Driving to a store or shop is symbolic for the drive to create or find choices.

**Physical Wellness**

*"I drive myself to find choices that create optimum health and bodily beauty."*

**Mental Wellness**

*"I drive myself to find choices of thought that will create a happy, balanced mind."*

**Career and Finances**

*"I drive myself to find choices to create more success in my career and finances."*

**Relationships**

*"I drive myself to find the choices I can make to have healthy, loving relationships."*

**Spirituality**

*"I drive myself to find the choices I can make to take me closer to my spiritual destiny."*

## Driving: Work
### Key Associations: motivation for activity

Driving to work is a metaphor for finding the motivation to put effort into some behavior or idea in order to achieve a definite result.

**Physical Wellness**

*"I drive myself to activities and behaviors that benefit my body."*

**Mental Wellness**

*"I drive myself to work toward a clear, focused, and balanced mind."*

**Career and Finances**

*"I drive myself to activities that will result in success and abundance."*

**Relationships**

*"I drive myself to work on developing my relationships."*

**Spirituality**

*"I drive myself toward activities that lead me toward spiritual achievement."*

## Eating (general)
### Key Associations: assimilation, thoughts, beliefs

The act of eating involves making choices and the assimilation of nutrients. Symbolically, any time we make ourselves receptive to information from whatever source, we assimilate the represented thoughts and beliefs thereof. So eating is a symbolic activity for the assimilation of ideas, thoughts, and beliefs, and also represents feeding an inner hunger for whatever we want to nourish us on a psychological level.

**Physical Wellness**

*"I assimilate every good nutrient that my body can use for optimum health."*
*"I satisfy my body's hunger for good and nutritious food."*

**Mental Wellness**

*"I feed my mind healthy and uplifting information."*
*"I choose to ingest beneficial thoughts and attitudes."*

**Career and Finances**

*"I assimilate ideas and beliefs that foster success and wealth."*
*"I satisfy my hunger for success in life."*

**Relationships**

*"I satisfy my appetite for loving and passionate relationships."*

**Spirituality**

*"I feed my soul what it needs to thrive."*
*"I feed on pure spirit."*
*"I satisfy my hunger to connect with the divine."*

## Eating: Fruit
### Key Associations: productivity, creativity, pleasure

Fruit, because it generally contains seeds, is a symbol for fertility, production, and creativity. Because it is sweet, it is also associated with the pleasurable aspects of life. Eating fruit, therefore, is symbolic for the intake of that which will make us productive and creative, as well as that which is pleasurable.

**Physical Wellness**

*"I take into my body what it needs to produce healthy cells."*

**Mental Wellness**

*"I take in ideas to produce healthy thoughts and creative ideas."*

**Career and Finances**

*"I assimilate creative ideas that can make my finances fruitful and multiply."*

**Relationships**

*"I take in the sweetness of my close relationships."*

**Spirituality**

*"I taste of the sweetness of the divine in my life."*

## Eating: Meat
### Key Associations: meaningful, satisfying

Because of its high protein content, eating meat is symbolic for assimilating that which is life-sustaining, hearty, and full of meaningful content.

**Physical Wellness**
*"I take in that which strengthens and nourishes my body."*

**Mental Wellness**
*"I nourish my mind with meaningful thoughts and ideas."*

**Career and Finances**
*"I provide myself with a satisfying and meaningful lifestyle."*

**Relationships**
*"I partake of hearty and meaningful relationships."*

**Spirituality**
*"My soul assimilates deep and satisfying spiritual concepts."*

## Eating: Vegetables
### Key Associations: health

Eating vegetables is symbolic for taking in that which is natural and health producing.

**Physical Wellness**

*"I assimilate vital nutrients into my body to produce optimal health."*

**Mental Wellness**

*"I feed my mind healthy thoughts that are natural to my mental well-being."*

**Career and Finances**

*"I feed myself with vital information to create success and abundance."*

**Relationships**

*"I assimilate the healthy love and friendship I receive from my relationships."*

**Spirituality**

*"I feed my soul what it needs to become healthier."*

Activities

## Entering a Doorway
### Key Associations: access, movement, initiation

Every doorway is a threshold from one place to another. Entering through a doorway, therefore, represents access to and movement from one place in our lives (or in consciousness) to another. To pass through a doorway is symbolic for being initiated into somewhere new, whether it's a new job, a new relationship, a new mind-set, or a new spiritual path. As you pass through any doorway, realize the new experiences in your life that you are ready for.

**Physical Wellness**

*"I enter into better health and wellness."*

*"I cross the threshold to complete recovery."*

**Mental Wellness**

*"I access new thoughts that take me into healthy areas of thought."*

*"I boldly enter new rooms of thought and feelings."*

**Career and Finances**

*"I cross the threshold to success and fortune."*

*"I enter into a new place in my career."*

**Relationships**

*"I access new levels of intimacy in my primary relationship."*

*"I step into new and beneficial relationships."*

**Spirituality**

*"I cross the threshold that leads to a fulfilled spirit."*

*"I walk through the doorway toward enlightenment."*

Activities

## Exercising
### Key Associations: clearing, releasing, strengthening

We exercise in order to keep the physical body fit and healthy, because our bodies are designed for movement. So it makes sense to recognize exercise as a symbolic activity for using effort to strengthen the mind through problem solving. We can use effort to stay sharp in business or to maintain good relationships; we can use regular discipline to strengthen our spiritual bodies. As you exercise, consider how you can use consistent effort to improve other areas of your life.

**Physical Wellness**

*"I use my effort to strengthen and heal my body."*

**Mental Wellness**

*"I make myself stronger and stronger, so I can handle things more easily."*
*"I exercise my mind with new thoughts and challenges to solve."*

**Career and Finances**

*"I use effort to build healthy finances."*
*"My endurance in career and financial matters increases daily."*

**Relationships**

*"I build and maintain strong relationships."*

**Spirituality**

*"I strengthen my spiritual connection through regular effort."*

Activities

## Exiting
### Key Associations: release, change

Any time we exit a place, we leave behind where we've been and move into other areas. This is symbolic of change in self or states of consciousness that involve letting go of that which has passed and moving on to matters at hand. Whenever you exit a room, a building, or an office, consider the importance of letting go of one area of thought or life so you can concentrate on another one.

**Physical Wellness**

*"I leave behind that which is unhealthy and concentrate on my body's needs."*
*"I create a division between my former habits to find healthier ways."*

**Mental Wellness**

*"I leave behind troubled places of thought and change my mind for the better."*
*"I create healthy divisions of thought to clear and organize my mind."*

**Career and Finances**

*"I change my career and finances for the better, and release the hold of past experiences."*

**Relationships**

*"I change my relationships for the better by letting go of past hurts."*

**Spirituality**

*"I bring myself into new experiences and let go of that which has passed."*

## Fueling a Car
### Key Associations: energy source, vitality

Your car (or other vehicle) is a symbol for the ego or the physical body. Fueling the car, therefore, is a metaphorical activity for providing the personality or the body with the motivation and energy it requires to work. This activity reminds us that we must replenish our supply with whatever physical or mental energy source will help us perform, whether it is nutritious food or self-empowering thoughts. In the spiritual sense, this activity can be a reminder or recognition of the divine source of life itself. As you fuel your car, consider what supplies you with energy in the area of your life for which you seek improvement.

**Physical Wellness**

*"I recognize the need to fuel my body with foods that provide me energy."*

**Mental Wellness**

*"I vitalize my mind with uplifting and empowering thoughts and emotions."*

**Career and Finances**

*"I fill myself with motivation to proceed with my goals."*

**Relationships**

*"I fill the engine of my heart with love as a source of energy in my relationships."*

**Spirituality**

*"I recognize the divine source of energy in all that I say and do."*

## Gardening (general)
### Key Associations: nurturing, growing

Gardening is an unparalleled symbolic activity for fostering inner growth and new ideas and for cultivating beneficial relationships. As you do your gardening, think about what you would like to see grow in your life.

**Physical Wellness**

*"I nurture and grow strong and healthy new cells in my body."*
*"I foster a strong, healthy, and beautiful body image."*
*"My body grows strong and healthy."*

**Mental Wellness**

*"I foster helpful and beautiful thoughts, beliefs, and attitudes."*
*"My mind grows stronger and healthier every day."*

**Career and Finances**

*"I nurture my finances to grow abundantly."*
*"I foster new and productive business ideas."*
*"I grow my wonderful career."*

**Relationships**

*"I take care of my relationships so they are healthy and beneficial."*
*"I foster beautiful and loving relationships."*

**Spirituality**

*"I grow and nurture inner wisdom."*
*"I foster my own spiritual growth."*

Activities

## Gardening: Fertilizing
### Key Associations: conditioning

Fertilizing the plants is a way of providing the best possible conditions for growth, so it is a symbol for providing the self with the best possible ideas and activities it needs for health and prosperity.

**Physical Wellness**

*"I provide my body with the best possible ingredients it needs to be healthy and strong."*

**Mental Wellness**

*"I provide my mind health-producing thoughts and attitudes."*

**Career and Finances**

*"I provide for myself all that I need to be successful and happy."*

**Relationships**

*"I give to my relationships all they need to grow strong and healthy."*

**Spirituality**

*"I give to my spirit all that it needs to grow healthy, happy, and strong."*

## Gardening: Planting Seeds
### Key Associations: new ideas, action, change

Seeds are a symbol for new ideas, creativity, and potential. Planting seeds is a metaphor for taking action on a new idea or plan leading to growth and change.

**Physical Wellness**

*"I plant the seeds of change toward a healthy, fit, and attractive body."*

**Mental Wellness**

*"I plant the seeds of change that create a happy, healthy mind-set."*

**Career and Finances**

*"I plant the seeds of change that grow into abundant success."*

**Relationships**

*"I plant the seeds that grow new and healthy relationships."*

**Spirituality**

*"I plant the seeds of change that help me grow and reach my destiny."*

Activities

# Gardening: Tilling Soil
## Key Associations: goal preparation

Tilling the soil is a preparation for the seeds that will be planted. This activity represents making necessary preparations for change and improvement.

**Physical Wellness**

*"I make the needed arrangements to help my body change."*

**Mental Wellness**

*"I prepare my mind for new ideas that will make it healthy, clear, and happy."*

**Career and Finances**

*"I make the needed arrangements to launch my career and financial goals."*

**Relationships**

*"I prepare my self so new and healthy relationships can sprout and grow."*

**Spirituality**

*"I arrange my life so I can help my spirit to grow."*

## Gardening: Watering
### Key Associations: vital care

Water is essential to a plant's survival, so watering represents providing essential care and attention to the self.

**Physical Wellness**

*"I provide my body vital care and what it needs to be healthy."*

**Mental Wellness**

*"I provide my mind the attention and care it needs to be healthy and happy."*

**Career and Finances**

*"I provide my career and finances vital attention and concern."*

**Relationships**

*"I attend to the vital needs of my relationships to sustain and nurture them."*

**Spirituality**

*"I provide vital care to ensure my inner growth and development."*

Activities

## Gardening: Weeding
### Key Associations: protecting

Weeding is a way to keep other plants from harming the growth of our gardens. This represents the regular removal and maintenance of ideas or behaviors that impede our development and improvement.

**Physical Wellness**

*"I weed out unproductive behaviors and attitudes that interfere with the health of my body."*

**Mental Wellness**

*"I weed out thoughts and ideas that harm my developing mind."*

**Career and Finances**

*"I weed out unproductive and negative behaviors and ideas that impede my success."*

**Relationships**

*"I weed out that which keeps my relationships from being healthy and mature."*

**Spirituality**

*"I weed out beliefs that are counterproductive to my spiritual growth."*

## Getting the Mail
### Key Associations: receptivity, inner communication

The mail is all about communication. Retrieving the mail is a marvelous metaphor for being receptive to the messages and wisdom of the inner self. When going to get the mail, think about what messages your body and mind might be sending you at this time. Concentrate on being receptive to important information and recognizing the difference between important messages and junk mail.

**Physical Wellness**
*"I am open and receptive to receiving the messages from my body."*

**Mental Wellness**
*"I retrieve the important messages my inner mind sends me."*

**Career and Finances**
*"I am receptive to ideas and information to further my career and finances."*

**Relationships**
*n/a*

**Spirituality**
*"I am receptive to divine wisdom and guidance."*

Activities

## Grooming
### Key Associations: beautification, presentation, preparation

Grooming is a symbolic activity for the beautification, presentation, and preparation of the self. It carries with it the idea of putting one's best foot forward (another apt metaphor). When we groom ourselves, we beautify and get ready to present ourselves in a respectable or favorable way. Beauty, of course, is a concept that transcends the physical realm and certainly transcends contemporary biases. Whatever is balanced and functional may be considered beautiful. When we speak of inner beauty or the beauty of our relationships, we think of a sense of order, balance, and prosperity.

**Physical Wellness**
>*"I feel healthy and attractive."*
>*"I am beautifully healthy, outside and in."*
>*"I create balance and beauty of mind and body."*

**Mental Wellness**
>*"I groom my thoughts to reflect order and clarity."*
>*"I beautify my thoughts."*

**Career and Finances**
>*"I groom myself for success and achievement."*
>*"I prepare and present myself in a balanced and dignified manner."*
>*"I present myself and my abilities beautifully."*

**Relationships**
>*"I beautify my relationships."*

**Spirituality**
>*"I beautify my soul even as I beautify my body."*
>*"I use my effort to beautify my spiritual self."*
>*"I groom myself for higher spiritual levels."*

## Home Improvement
### Key Associations: self-improvement

Any kind of home improvement, whether it's painting or wallpapering, recarpeting or putting in tiles, is a symbolic activity for self-improvement. The home is a symbol for the self as a whole; therefore, improving the home is a metaphor for improving the mind, personality, and body. As you work on your home, realize that improving yourself makes your life function better and beautifies your outlook and circumstances.

**Physical Wellness**

*"I repair and enhance this aspect of myself."*
*"I make changes and improve my physical condition."*

**Mental Wellness**

*"I improve my thoughts and repair my mind."*
*"I enhance my emotional self and make improvements where needed."*

**Career and Finances**

*"I improve my relationship with money."*
*"I repair my feelings about my career and finances."*

**Relationships**

*"I improve the quality of my relationships by improving myself."*

**Spirituality**

*"I improve my relationship with my spiritual self."*

# Ironing Clothes
## Key Associations: correcting, perfecting

Ironing clothes is primarily performed in order to smooth out the wrinkles, thus returning them to their most perfect appearance and function. Metaphorically, ironing represents correcting or perfecting the self in some way—or perhaps even aspects of our relationships. Common sayings such as "we ironed out our problems" serve to highlight the deeper meaning of this symbolic task. When ironing, recognize your innate patience and intelligence to "iron out" your problems, whatever they may be. Notice your sense of satisfaction as you watch the wrinkles vanish.

**Physical Wellness**
*"I iron out my health issues and restore the natural perfection of my body."*

**Mental Wellness**
*"I iron out my mental and emotional issues and restore my mind to perfect balance."*
*"I smooth away stressful thoughts and emotions."*

**Career and Finances**
*"I iron out my financial challenges."*
*"I iron out career challenges to make my work rewarding and productive."*

**Relationships**
*"I iron out the challenges in my relationships that they may be harmonious and happy."*

**Spirituality**
*"The divine corrects and perfects my soul to express beauty, love, and power."*

Activities

## Knitting
### Key Associations: productive patterns

Knitting is a creative skill used to form useful garments made up of patterns of yarn. This is a powerful metaphor for promoting the formation of patterns of thought and behavior to create a beautiful and productive life. As you knit, recognize that you have the power and ability to create new and healthy patterns in your life to affect your target areas, and that with skill, attention, and persistence you can have the result you want.

**Physical Wellness**

*"I use skill and persistence to form healthy patterns of behavior to establish a beautiful and fully functional body."*

**Mental Wellness**

*"I form beautiful and functional patterns of thought to establish a powerful and healthy mind."*

**Career and Finances**

*"I form productive patterns of behavior to establish a productive career and healthy income."*

**Relationships**

*"I form beautiful patterns of behavior and thought that construct loving and healthy relationships."*

**Spirituality**

*"I construct wonderful patterns in my life and my mind that reflect the beauty of the divine within."*

*"The divine creates in me beautiful patterns of thought and behavior that express the fruit of the spirit."*

## Lawn Mowing
### Key Associations: maintenance, control

Mowing the grass is symbolic for keeping thoughts and behavior under control. The yard represents a natural yet cultivated field of thoughts, emotions, and behaviors rooted in our intrinsic human nature. The greenness of the grass is a metaphor for the life-possessing quality of thoughts and feelings. And as cutting the lawn is an activity that must be performed with some regularity, so too must our bodies, thoughts, and activities be maintained and in check if we are to keep our lives in order.

**Physical Wellness**

*"I maintain my body to keep it healthy and under control."*

**Mental Wellness**

*"I cultivate and control my thoughts to be beautiful and productive."*
*"I keep my thoughts and feelings from getting out of control."*

**Career and Finances**

*"I control my finances with regular upkeep and attention."*

**Relationships**

*"I cultivate and maintain healthy, beautiful relationships."*

**Spirituality**

*"I cultivate and maintain my spirituality."*

Activities

## Listening
### Key Associations: understanding

When we listen to anyone or anything, we use our attention to hear and understand whatever is being communicated. Understanding ourselves and others is a major key to all self-advancement. As you listen to anything in your life, realize that there are many messages life has for you if you are ready and willing to understand them.

**Physical Wellness**

*"I listen to the important messages from my body."*

**Mental Wellness**

*"I listen and understand the messages from my inner mind."*

**Career and Finances**

*"I listen to sound financial advice and heed it."*

**Relationships**

*"I listen and understand what those close to me have to say to me."*

**Spirituality**

*"I listen carefully to the inner voice of the divine."*
*"I understand the messages of my true self."*

## Office Chores
### Key Associations: administration, organization

Whether at a business or home office, chores such as filing and stapling are symbolic for organizing and taking care of the details of the "business" of everyday life. So much of what we need to do for our bodies, our minds, our finances, our relationships, and even our souls has to do with the details. So while the big picture and glamour of our goals is certainly important, office chores symbolically remind us that the details in self-administration and organization cannot be overlooked.

**Physical Wellness**

*"I address the details of my body's needs to achieve maximum health."*

**Mental Wellness**

*"I organize my thoughts in detail to have a healthy and balanced mind."*

**Career and Finances**

*"I address the details and organization of my career and financial goals."*

**Relationships**

*"I address the details of my behavior in maintaining healthy relationships."*

**Spirituality**

*"I recognize the everyday details and organization required to attain advanced levels of the soul."*

## Paying Bills
### Key Associations: offering, atonement, responsibility

Paying bills is an activity of fulfilling one's financial obligations based on services or products already provided or obtained. It is a symbolic activity for the reconciliation or equalization of some aspect of the self or of relationships—the give-and-take of life. This should not be viewed as something bad or negative, but simply a part of the spoken and unspoken contracts we make with ourselves and with others. Paying a bill is simply a means of balancing the scales, so to speak. As you pay your bills, recognize areas of your life as a series of "checks and balances."

**Physical Wellness**

*"I give my body what it needs to rebalance itself."*
*"I pay my body back for good health by providing nutrition and rest."*
*"I pay my body back with loving care for serving me well."*

**Mental Wellness**

*"I balance my mental checkbook to maintain order and wellness."*

**Career and Finances**

*"I pay my bill so others continue to provide me with what I want and need."*

**Relationships**

*"I balance my relationships with due effort and attention."*

**Spirituality**

*"I acknowledge the undeviating justice in the circumstances of my life."*
*"I mindfully balance the scales to create positive karma."*

## Pet Care (general)
### Key Associations: nurturing and refining instincts

Symbolically, pets are extensions of the domesticated, instinctual self. Thus, when we feed, groom, or show affection to our pets, these are symbolic activities for strengthening, nurturing, or training traits within the self that are animal-like. When taking care of a pet in general, realize that you are simultaneously addressing the animal aspect of your own nature. This part of you responds to basic care, love, and attention when it is provided, just like your pet does.

**Physical Wellness**
*"I nurture my instincts for self-healing."*
*"I pay attention to the needs of my bodily instincts to preserve my health."*

**Mental Wellness**
*"I support and love my mental and emotional instincts, which serve me well."*
*"I nurture and train my emotional instincts to be happy."*

**Career and Finances**
*"I support and train my instincts to become more successful in my career."*

**Relationships**
*"I pay attention to my relationship instincts."*
*"I train my instincts to serve me well in my relationships."*

**Spirituality**
*"I love and support my instinctual nature as part of the divine plan."*
*"I train and refine my animal instincts to support my spiritual life."*

## Pet Care: Birds
### Key Associations: freedom, joy, spirituality

Because of their ability to sing and fly, birds are associated with freedom-loving instincts as well as an innate sense of joy and spirituality. When caring for your bird, recognize your own instincts to be free and to experience the natural joy of existence in whatever area you are attempting to enhance.

**Physical Wellness**

*"I nurture the natural joy and freedom of a healthy body."*

**Mental Wellness**

*"I nurture my inner sense of joy."*

**Career and Finances**

*"I nurture my joyful desire for financial freedom."*

**Relationships**

*n/a*

**Spirituality**

*"I support and love my innate spirit of freedom and divine joy."*

## Pet Care: Cats
### Key Associations: curiosity, intuition, independence, sensuality

Cats have many defining characteristics that have parallels to human instincts. Among them are curiosity, intuition, independence, and sensuality. When taking care of your cat, consider how nurturing some of the above-mentioned attributes in yourself might enhance and improve your life.

**Physical Wellness**

*"I nurture my physical agility and sensual nature."*

**Mental Wellness**

*"I care for and support my natural curiosity/independence/sensuality."*

**Career and Finances**

*"I foster my intuition in all of my financial and career affairs."*

**Relationships**

*"I recognize my intuition about people and relationships."*

**Spirituality**

*"I love and support my independent spirit."*

## Pet Care: Dogs
### Key Associations: loyalty, courage, friendship

Dogs are well-known for their kinship, courage, and loyalty if they are treated well. When caring for your dog, think about your own innate courage and sense of loyalty. Realize that you are your own best friend and you should treat yourself as such.

**Physical Wellness**

*"I nurture my body, and it is my loyal companion in life."*

**Mental Wellness**

*"I love and care for my innate courage and sense of loyalty."*

**Career and Finances**

*n/a*

**Relationships**

*"I nurture friendliness and loyalty in how I relate to others."*

**Spirituality**

*"I foster courage and loyalty to serve the divine."*

## Pet Care: Fish
### Key Associations: emotional freedom, inner nature

Water is a symbol for the emotional and spiritual self. Because fish are at home in the water, they are associated with emotional freedom and the inner self. When tending to your fish, recognize that you possess and value a deep emotional and/or spiritual nature that goes beyond the surface of what you might display to others.

**Physical Wellness**

*n/a*

**Mental Wellness**

*"I nurture my inner self and emotional expression."*
*"I care about and develop a relationship with my inner feelings."*

**Career and Finances**

*n/a*

**Relationships**

*"I connect with my deep feelings about the world and my relationships."*

**Spirituality**

*"I love and nurture my deep spiritual self."*

## Pet Care: Horses
### Key Associations: power, speed, elegance

Horses are animals of great power, speed, and elegance. Thus, they represent human potential, a fast mind, and an elegant demeanor. And because humans have used them as a means of transportation, they can even represent the physical body. When taking care of your horse, recognize your own sense of power and elegance, inside and out.

**Physical Wellness**

*"I take care and love my physical body and all of its power and elegance."*

**Mental Wellness**

*"I nurture a fast and powerful mind and balanced, elegant emotions."*

**Career and Finances**

*"I support my own power and diligence to become more successful."*

**Relationships**

*"I nurture my sense of elegance and power in my relationships with others."*

**Spirituality**

*"I support the power and elegance of my inner spirit."*

## Pet Care: Mice (Rodents)
### Key Associations: gentleness, lovability

Mice and similar small rodents represent what is simply gentle and sweet. Every human being has a sweet, lovable nature, though it sometimes goes unrecognized. When caring for your mouse, recognize your own innate lovability.

**Physical Wellness**

*"I love and take care of myself."*

**Mental Wellness**

*"I recognize and nurture what is lovable about me."*

**Career and Finances**

*n/a*

**Relationships**

*"I am naturally lovable and gentle."*

**Spirituality**

*"I foster my gentle and lovable spirit."*

Activities

## Pet Care: Rabbits
### Key Associations: peacefulness, gentleness, creativity

Rabbits are associated with a gentle and peaceful nature as well as potential fertility, as they can reproduce quickly and voluminously. Fertility, in the metaphorical sense, refers to creativity, the rapid formation and reproduction of thoughts. When caring for your rabbit, consider how you might foster your own peaceful nature or how the fostering of new ideas might lead you to a more successful life.

**Physical Wellness**

*"I nurture the peacefulness within to create and maintain a healthy body."*

**Mental Wellness**

*"I nurture a gentle and peaceful mind."*
*"I nurture my creative mind and love the plentitude of ideas that come forth."*

**Career and Finances**

*"I pay attention to many new ideas to multiply my finances."*
*"I nurture my ability to form many new ideas to advance my career."*

**Relationships**

*"I cultivate a gentle, loving nature in my close relationships."*

**Spirituality**

*"I love and appreciate my gentle, peaceful self."*

Activities

## Pet Care: Snakes
### Key Associations: life, change

Snakes have been seen for centuries as a mystic symbol for life and energy. Because they shed their skin, they also represent the power of transformation. When caring for your pet snake, recognize your aliveness and that you have the natural ability to change and transform yourself.

**Physical Wellness**

*"I nurture my living body to change in healthy ways."*

**Mental Wellness**

*"I nurture my living mind as it changes and develops in healthy ways."*

**Career and Finances**

*n/a*

**Relationships**

*"I cultivate lively relationships that change and transform."*

**Spirituality**

*"I nurture my living spirit that transforms and renews me."*

## Plugging in an Appliance
### Key Associations: connection, power

Plugging an electrical device into an outlet provides the power needed to perform its intended function. This is a symbol for connecting with people, ideas, beliefs, and emotions that might serve us in our self-improvement efforts. When plugging in a device of any kind, recognize your own ability to connect with yourself and others to accomplish what you need. Understand that power for accomplishing your goals is available; all you have to do is connect with it.

**Physical Wellness**

*"I connect with that which I need to make my body more healthy and powerful."*

**Mental Wellness**

*"I connect with ideas and attitudes that empower me."*

**Career and Finances**

*"I connect with powerful ideas and people who empower my career and further my financial gain."*

**Relationships**

*"I connect with and am empowered by loving, healthy relationships."*

**Spirituality**

*"I am connected with the divine and all like-minded, empowering individuals."*

## Polishing (general)
### Key Associations: beautification, purification, refinement

Polishing removes tarnish or debris to beautify an object. Thus, polishing is a metaphor for the purification or beautification of some aspect of the mind, behavior, or life. Generally, polishing is about restoration, bringing out and refining the existing beauty of an object, rather than adding to or covering it up. Polishing can also refer to taking something old and making it useful again, and this can apply to our skills as suggested by a saying like, "I'd better polish up on my knowledge." As you polish an object, consider what hidden abilities and knowledge you have and how to refine it to improve your life.

**Physical Wellness**
*"I refine my body to express beauty and health."*

**Mental Wellness**
*"I bring out the beauty of pure thought and emotion."*
*"I purify and beautify my inner thoughts and feelings."*

**Career and Finances**
*"I polish up on my knowledge of my job and finances."*

**Relationships**
*"I restore my relationships with love and attention."*

**Spirituality**
*"The divine refines and polishes my soul to bring out its most beautiful expression."*

Activities

162

## Polishing: Floors
### Key Associations: foundation refinement

Polishing a floor is symbolic for conditioning and refining the foundation of self.

**Physical Wellness**
*"I refine my physical condition to provide optimum beauty and efficiency."*

**Mental Wellness**
*"I refine my basic thoughts and beliefs."*

**Career and Finances**
*"I polish up on my basic understanding of money and my work."*

**Relationships**
*"I refine the foundation of love and trust in my relationships."*

**Spirituality**
*"I refine my core beliefs about life and the divine."*

Activities

## Polishing: Gold
### Key Associations: value, special

Polishing gold is a metaphor for the careful treatment of whatever we place high value on.

**Physical Wellness**

*"I give special care to my precious and valuable physical body."*

**Mental Wellness**

*"I give special care to the condition of my mind."*

**Career and Finances**

*"I give special care to my career and aspirations."*

**Relationships**

*"I give special care to my golden relationships."*

**Spirituality**

*"I give special care to my spiritual self."*

## Polishing: Shoes
### Key Associations: preparation, self-image

Polishing shoes is a metaphor for the special care needed as you prepare to make choices. Additionally it represents a good self-image, the excellence revealed in strong personal foundations.

**Physical Wellness**

*"I prepare to make the best possible choices that will lead in the direction of optimal wellness."*

*"I clean and polish my physical self-image."*

**Mental Wellness**

*"I clean and polish the foundations that lead to ideal mental clarity and health."*

**Career and Finances**

*"I clean and shine my self-image that I may successfully present myself to the world."*

**Relationships**

*n/a*

**Spirituality**

*"I prepare myself for my spiritual journey."*

## Polishing: Silver
### Key Associations: subconscious refinement

Polishing silver is a metaphor for giving special care and treatment to the inner mind, the subconscious.

**Physical Wellness**

*"I give special care to the functioning of my physical body."*

**Mental Wellness**

*"I care for and refine the functions and inner thoughts of my mind."*

**Career and Finances**

*n/a*

**Relationships**

*n/a*

**Spirituality**

*"I give special attention and support to my inner self."*

# Polishing: Wood
## Key Associations: refining the natural self

Polishing wood is symbolic for the refinement of the natural functions and expressions of the self.

**Physical Wellness**

*"I refine the functions and appearance of my natural body."*

**Mental Wellness**

*"I refine the natural thoughts and feelings of my mind to be beautiful and functional."*

**Career and Finances**

*n/a*

**Relationships**

*"I refine my natural behavior in relationships that they may become more beautiful."*

**Spirituality**

*"The divine refines my natural self to express beauty and love."*

## Pouring Liquid
### Key Associations: expressing, channeling

Pouring a liquid from one container to another is symbolic for expressing emotions, as noted in familiar sayings like, "He poured his heart out to me." It also can denote the idea of channeling emotional or spiritual power into a new endeavor. When you pour a liquid of any kind, realize your ability to express and channel your emotions into your target areas.

**Physical Wellness**

> *"I channel my emotions into the well-being of my body."*
> *"I pour over my joy of having a healthy, attractive body."*

**Mental Wellness**

> *"I healthily express my feelings and channel them in productive ways."*

**Career and Finances**

> *"I channel my desire into creating success and abundance."*

**Relationships**

> *"I pour more love into my close relationships."*

**Spirituality**

> *"I channel love and desire into my spiritual activities."*
> *"I channel love to and from the divine source."*

## Recycling
### Key Associations: transformation

Scientists tell us that energy is never destroyed, but simply changes states: it transforms. Recycling trash (for example, paper, plastic, and metal) is a metaphor for recognizing that all of our experiences, even the ones we'd like to throw away, can be transformed into learning experiences to make our lives better. When dealing with recycling, recognize that you have the power to transmute your life and that nothing need be considered truly a waste.

**Physical Wellness**

*"I transform my body to provide greater health, functionality, and beauty."*

**Mental Wellness**

*"I transform my mind with renewed thoughts that cultivate peace and happiness."*

**Career and Finances**

*"I transform my career into renewed and more profitable ways."*

**Relationships**

*"I transform my relationships to renew them in mutually beneficial ways."*

**Spirituality**

*"The divine transforms me into more useful and loving expressions."*

## Riding in an Elevator
### Key Associations: guided change, understanding

Riding an elevator or escalator is an automated or assisted means of going up or down. Symbolically, this activity represents inner guidance leading to higher wisdom (going up) or deeper understanding (going down) for some issue or problem. As you get on the elevator/escalator, recognize the inner wisdom and guidance that is within you to help you get to the next level of self-improvement.

**Physical Wellness**
*"I am guided to the next level of bodily health."*
*"I listen to the inner wisdom and guidance coming from my body."*

**Mental Wellness**
*"I am guided to greater and deeper levels of self-understanding."*
*"I am guided to the next level of mental and emotional health."*

**Career and Finances**
*"I am guided toward greater levels of success in my career and finances."*
*"I am guided toward greater/deeper understanding of financial matters."*

**Relationships**
*"I am guided toward greater/deeper levels of love and friendship."*

**Spirituality**
*"I am guided toward higher/deeper levels of spiritual growth."*

## Schoolwork
### Key Associations: learning, understanding

Going to school and all related schoolwork is about learning and gaining knowledge. The idea of learning and understanding can be applied to all areas of self-improvement. When dealing with classes, schoolwork, or study of any kind, consider how the school of life is giving you knowledge and insight to help you improve in your target areas.

**Physical Wellness**

*"I learn how to become healthier, fitter, and more attractive."*

*"I school myself in the ways of the body to keep it healthy and vital."*

**Mental Wellness**

*"I gain knowledge and understanding of my mental processes to become more centered and happy."*

*"I am a student of the mind to gain more insight about myself."*

**Career and Finances**

*"I gain knowledge and understanding to help me become more successful."*

**Relationships**

*"I study my own behavior so I can attract and maintain healthy relationships."*

**Spirituality**

*"I am a student in the school of life, making me a wiser soul."*

# Sewing
## Key Associations: creation, restoration, joining

Sewing is a metaphor for creating, joining, or restoring aspects of ourselves or our lives. For example, these aspects may be of a physical nature, as in the restoration of physical or mental health, a relationship, or the creation of a business venture. The stitching that epitomizes the act of sewing carries with it the idea of binding things in a useful and attractive fashion.

**Physical Wellness**
*"My body restores itself to perfect function and beauty."*

**Mental Wellness**
*"I join together healthy and uplifting patterns of thought."*
*"I restore my thoughts and emotions to perfect equilibrium."*
*"I create wonderful new thought patterns."*

**Career and Finances**
*"I create a cohesive and thriving career."*
*"I create a well-made business."*

**Relationships**
*"I restore my relationships."*
*"I stitch my relationships together with love and attention."*

**Spirituality**
*"The divine binds me to my spiritual path."*

## Sexual Activity
### Key Associations: connection, love, pleasure

Sexual activity with others or even oneself (as in masturbation) is symbolic for making an intimate connection with some aspect of the inner self or even with the divine. For instance, sharing sexual behavior with a man is a symbolic activity for achieving union with our masculine powers or traits; whereas sex with a woman represents connecting with our feminine aspects. Sex with oneself can represent self-love and self-connection. In the spiritual sense, sexual acts may be seen as sacred, with one's partner representing the masculine or feminine aspect of divinity. There is also, of course, a strong association of sex with the ability to both give and receive pleasure.

### Physical Wellness
*"I recognize the joy and pleasure of my physical senses."*
*"I embrace my physical desires with joy and enthusiasm."*

### Mental Wellness
*"I make intimate contact with the masculine/feminine side within."*
*"I love myself and experience pleasure on all levels of my mind."*

### Career and Finances
*"I make an intimate connection with my ability to make things happen."*
*"I make an intimate connection with my ability to receive good things."*

### Relationships
*"I enjoy my ability to give and receive pleasure."*

### Spirituality
*"I recognize and make contact with the divine masculine/feminine in my partner."*
*"I establish a union with the divine."*

## Shopping
### Key Associations: searching, gathering, making choices

Shopping may be viewed as a metaphor for searching and gathering that which is needed in our lives, whether it's a search for a spiritual path or a relationship, or a gathering of one's thoughts on some matter. Shopping implies using discretion to make appropriate choices. For instance, the well-known saying "you'd better shop around" emphasizes the idea that a thorough search is recommended to find the best possible relationship. But discretion and making choices apply not only to relationships, but to all other life areas as well. As you go shopping, consider that you are in control of the choices you make in your life and that these choices affect your quality of life.

**Physical Wellness**
*"I find the best resources for my physical health."*

**Mental Wellness**
*"I carefully choose for myself what to think and how to feel."*

**Career and Finances**
*"I search for the best choices to make in my career."*
*"I gather all of the appropriate information to make financial choices."*

**Relationships**
*"I search for the best in all of my relationships."*
*"I gather excellent people to me."*
*"I shop around for the best new relationships."*

**Spirituality**
*"I search for the tools and nourishment I need for my spiritual well-being."*

174

## Sitting
### Key Associations: self-reflection, patience, comfort

When we sit down, we change from an active state of motion to one of repose. This is a metaphor for becoming comfortable, reflective, and patient with ourselves and our circumstances. Whenever you sit down, realize that although effort and activity are required for change, part of the formula for success is in knowing how and when to relax from conscious effort, and in so doing, allowing the inner self to carry on the work.

**Physical Wellness**
*"I relax and patiently reflect on the physical improvements I am undergoing."*

**Mental Wellness**
*"I give my mind opportunity to relax, reflect, and become balanced and clear."*

**Career and Finances**
*"I afford myself opportunities to relax and reflect on my career and financial goals and circumstances."*

**Relationships**
*"I relax and reflect on what is good about my relationships."*

**Spirituality**
*"I am comfortable and patient about my spiritual journey and growth."*

Activities

## Sleeping
### Key Associations: restoration, processing

When we sleep or rest, our bodies repair themselves and our minds process thoughts and feelings from the previous day. So going to sleep is a symbolic activity for the processing of life issues and for recovery from the fatigue and wounds of life, so to speak. The saying "let's sleep on it" expresses that some things require careful thought that can only take place over time. Sleep also carries with it the idea of the cessation of conscious worry or effort. As you prepare to go to sleep, recognize your natural ability to process all that occurs in your life and restore yourself to optimum wellness.

**Physical Wellness**
*"My body repairs itself as I sleep and makes me healthier and stronger."*

**Mental Wellness**
*"I process all thoughts and emotions to create total mental wellness."*

**Career and Finances**
*"I carefully consider and process all financial and career decisions before committing to them."*

**Relationships**
*n/a*

**Spirituality**
*"I rest in the arms of the divine."*
*"I rest my life on the foundation of eternal being."*

Activities

## Sports and Games (general)
### Key Associations: skills, goals, rules

On the surface, playing is associated with leisure, but all games and sports contain metaphors for daily life. Playing an organized game is, in general, a metaphor for dealing with the spoken or unspoken rules of life and relationships. When playing a game or sport, realize that areas of life also contain rules, and consider how your application of those rules might best serve your self-improvement efforts.

**Physical Wellness**
*"I follow the rules that lead to greater health and fitness."*
*"I play the game to achieve perfect health and wellness."*

**Mental Wellness**
*"I have the mental and emotional skills to play the game of life."*
*"I internalize the rules of thought to achieve and maintain mental balance."*

**Career and Finances**
*"I master the money game to achieve financial success."*
*"I sharpen my skills to play well in my career."*

**Relationships**
*"I recognize the rules of good relationships."*

**Spirituality**
*"I recognize and play within the rules of cosmic law."*
*"I enhance my spiritual skills to win the game of spiritual advancement."*

## Sports and Games: Archery
### Key Associations: focus, accuracy, persistence

Archery requires tremendous focus and persistence in order to accurately hit the target. This sport is symbolic for the persistence and focus required for achievement in life. While practicing archery, think about the areas of your life in which you can summon your focus and persistence in order to achieve a specific goal. Note that an archer always has a specific target. Likewise, we must have specific goals if we intend to achieve them.

**Physical Wellness**

*"I focus on the health and wellness of my body until I achieve it."*

*"I persistently make my body stronger and healthier."*

**Mental Wellness**

*"I focus on achieving a strong and healthy mind-set."*

**Career and Finances**

*"I focus on the goal of my career until I have attained it."*

*"I aim for the target of abundant financial health."*

**Relationships**

*"I persistently aim for loving and mutually satisfying relationships."*

**Spirituality**

*"I focus on the spiritual disciplines to achieve my divine goals."*

## Sports and Games: Baseball
### Key Associations: achievement, teamwork

Baseball contains many metaphors. Since it's played as a team, it's associated with working cohesively with a group, being "a team player." On the individual level, the saying "step up to plate" suggests the idea of taking initiative, and the saying "hit it out of the ballpark" is a metaphor for success. There is also the idea of "playing the field," a metaphor for considering many options. When you play baseball as a batter, think of the opportunities you have in life to achieve your goals, and remember that not every hit must be a home run to ultimately succeed or win. And even if you "strike out" there will be another time "at bat." When playing in the field, consider the ideas of cooperation among peers and parts of your own mind and personality.

**Physical Wellness**
*"I step up to the plate to make my health better."*
*"I cooperate with health-providing sources to strike out body illness."*

**Mental Wellness**
*"I take a swing at every opportunity to improve my mental health."*
*"I cooperate with health-providing sources to strike out mental illness."*

**Career and Finances**
*"I take a swing at opportunities to advance my career and finances."*
*"I work with all allies to strike out debt."*

**Relationships**
*"I step up to the plate to make my attitude in relationships better."*
*"I work with my partner to defeat negative influences and dissention."*

**Spirituality**
*"I step up to the plate to advance my spiritual walk."*

## Sports and Games: Basketball
### Key Associations: cooperation, persistence, opportunity

Basketball requires teamwork as well as thwarting the constant barrage of opponents. It is also a high-scoring game, requiring unrelenting motivation on the part of players. When you play basketball, realize all the forces you must work with and the ones you must work against to achieve your goals. Think about how an unrelenting attitude can overcome all obstacles in your life. Also think about what it means to "take your shot."

**Physical Wellness**
*"I unrelentingly work toward better health and wellness."*

**Mental Wellness**
*"I overcome all ideas that keep me from a peaceful mind."*

**Career and Finances**
*"I persist in striving for my financial and career goals."*

**Relationships**
*"I work with my relationships to overcome disharmony."*

**Spirituality**
*"I unrelentingly work toward the improvement of my spiritual life."*

## Sports and Games: Bicycling
### Key Associations: balance, self-power

Bicycling requires balance and using personal effort to pedal. Thus, this activity is a metaphor for any areas where we can be more balanced, areas that require our personal motivation and attention. As you are bicycling, realize how many of your goals rely on your motivation as well as your ability to balance things in your life in order to be successful.

**Physical Wellness**

*"I am motivated to have a healthy and balanced diet."*
*"I am self-motivated to ride myself to fitness and health."*

**Mental Wellness**

*"I am motivated to have a healthy and balanced mind."*

**Career and Finances**

*"I successfully balance my finances."*
*"I am self-motivated to achieve in my profession."*

**Relationships**

*"I find the perfect balance in my relationships."*

**Spirituality**

*"I am motivated to work my way toward my spiritual goals."*

## Sports and Games: Boating/Sailing
### Key Associations: self-direction

Boating or sailing involves successful navigation through a body of water. A natural body of water is, among other things, a symbol for life. So steering a boat is a symbol for purposeful movement through life circumstances to reach a goal. When boating or sailing, think about where you are going in your life.

**Physical Wellness**

*"I successfully navigate my way to perfect health."*

**Mental Wellness**

*"I take my thoughts and feelings in the direction I want them to go."*

**Career and Finances**

*"I navigate my career toward greater success."*
*"I chart my course to experience financial abundance."*

**Relationships**

*"I set my course to experience wonderful relationships."*

**Spirituality**

*"I navigate through the waters of life on my divine journey."*
*"I set the course of my life toward lands of the spirit."*

Activities

## Sports and Games: Cards
### Key Associations: mastery of cycles, self-control, opportunity

To win, many card games require understanding how to ride the tides of fortune, which is indeed a skill. While luck may not be controllable, the prediction of trends and how we temper ourselves are very much within our control. Sayings like "if you play your cards right" reveal the metaphor of taking calculated advantage of opportunities when they arise. When playing cards, realize that your reactions and responses in life are very much in your control and can be mastered to optimize what fortune brings you.

**Physical Wellness**

*"I recognize my body's rhythms and work with them to sustain wellness."*

**Mental Wellness**

*"I work with the rhythms of thought and emotion to gain mental mastery."*
*"I learn to control my thoughts and emotions to win my happiness."*

**Career and Finances**

*"I recognize the trends in my profession to achieve success."*
*"I control my finances and utilize them to my greatest benefit."*

**Relationships**

*"I am in control of my emotional reactions in relationships."*

**Spirituality**

*"I learn the lessons of spiritual rhythm and self-mastery."*

## Sports and Games: Checkers/Chess
### Key Associations: intellect, planning

Checkers and chess often require the formulation of strategies and a keen mind for victory. Thus they build intellectual prowess as well as the patterns needed to form effective strategies in life. As you sit down to play chess or checkers, remind yourself that you are building mental skills and can apply them toward important pursuits.

**Physical Wellness**

*"I use my keen intellect to become healthier."*

**Mental Wellness**

*"I have a keen intellect and the ability to form effective strategies in life."*

**Career and Finances**

*"I use my sharp mind and planning skills to create financial abundance."*

*"I use my powerful intellect and sense of strategy to advance my career."*

**Relationships**

*"I use my intellect and planning skills to create and sustain good relationships."*

**Spirituality**

*"I call upon my intellect and powers of deduction to advance my spiritual goals."*

184

## Sports and Games: Dancing
### Key Associations: self-expression, participation in life, joy

Dancing is a rhythmic movement that expresses emotion. It can be highly structured or freestyle. It is a marvelous metaphor for the movement and cycles of life and our ability to participate in them and express through them. When dancing, realize your participation in your life and circumstances. Consider what you'd like to express.

**Physical Wellness**

*"I participate with my body and its rhythms to express health."*

**Mental Wellness**

*"My thoughts express beautiful and balanced patterns."*

**Career and Finances**

*"I express abundance and success through my career and finances."*

**Relationships**

*"I participate in the joyful dance of relationships."*

**Spirituality**

*"I joyfully participate in the divine dance of life."*

Activities

## Sports and Games: Fishing
### Key Associations: knowledge, insight

Fishing represents a search for knowledge and insight. Catching fish represents acquiring knowledge or insight. This might be knowledge about the self or about some specific area of life. Fishing can also be a metaphor for seeking something new, such as a relationship. When you go fishing, consider what kind of insights might serve your current life purposes at this time. Think also about the metaphorical value of waiting and the anticipation that is inherent in this sport.

### Physical Wellness
*"I seek and gain knowledge leading to the total wellness of my body."*
*"I fish for understanding to restore my body to health."*

### Mental Wellness
*"I search my inner mind for the truth about myself."*
*"I seek insight about my true thoughts and feelings."*

### Career and Finances
*"I fish for new ideas about how to increase my finances."*
*"I seek and find ways to improve my career."*

### Relationships
*"I seek insight for enhancing my relationships."*
*"I cast my line to find new and happy relationships."*

### Spirituality
*"I cast my line to catch spiritual insight."*
*"I search for spiritual truths and catch them when they surface."*

Activities

## Sports and Games: Football
### Key Associations: cooperation, initiative

Football is associated with the cooperation with others needed to achieve success. It also requires initiative to be taken amidst opposition, which is also needed in other areas of life. As you play football, realize that you must learn cooperation not only with others but also with the various aspects of your own psyche in order to achieve your goals. Also think what action steps you might take in order to advance toward your ultimate goal.

**Physical Wellness**

*"I cooperate with my health providers to achieve perfect health."*

*"I work with all of my inner resources to take action toward total wellness."*

**Mental Wellness**

*"All aspects of my mind and personality cooperate to achieve the goal of mental happiness and balance."*

**Career and Finances**

*"I work well with others who help me achieve my financial and career goals."*

**Relationships**

*"I take initiative to reach the goal of happy and beneficial relationships."*

**Spirituality**

*"I cooperate with the divine to attain spiritual growth and mastery."*

## Sports and Games: Gambling
### Key Associations: self-control, risk taking

Controlled gambling involves calculated risk taking, patience, and taking advantage of opportunities and probable (or possible) outcomes. Self-control is often critical. When gambling, realize you are affirming your courage to take risks in life in order to receive a possible reward.

**Physical Wellness**

*n/a*

**Mental Wellness**

*n/a*

**Career and Finances**

*"I take calculated risks to advance my career and finances."*

**Relationships**

*"I take controlled risks in relationships to make them rich and strong."*

**Spirituality**

*"I courageously risk my life path on my spiritual principles."*

## Sports and Games: Golf
### Key Associations: motivation, concentration

Golf is associated with the skill and concentration required to play it well. The "driving" club, for example, can be thought of as a metaphor for your drive to succeed with your life goals, particularly those that seem far from completion. Using a putter is a metaphor for concentrating on the final phase toward the completion of a goal. As you are golfing, think about how you'd like to concentrate on your life goals.

**Physical Wellness**

*"I have the long-term drive to make my body strong and healthy."*
*"I concentrate on the details that lead me to perfect wellness."*

**Mental Wellness**

*"I focus on the wellness of mind and the green of balanced emotions."*

**Career and Finances**

*"I concentrate on my long-term and short-term financial goals."*

**Relationships**

*"I have the long-term drive for lasting and satisfying relationships."*

**Spirituality**

*"I focus on my ultimate spiritual goal and drive myself toward it."*

Activities

## Sports and Games: Jump Rope
### Key Associations: timing, endurance

Jumping rope requires tremendous timing and endurance, if one is jumping for any significant length of time. Timing and endurance are important for success with many things. So as you jump rope, realize how your timing and persistence in your goals may be important factors for their attainment.

**Physical Wellness**

*"I persistently work with the natural rhythms of my body to maintain wellness."*

**Mental Wellness**

*"I work and have fun with my natural, mental, and emotional rhythms."*

**Career and Finances**

*"I work with my timing to advance my career and financial worth."*

**Relationships**

*"I negotiate the natural rhythms in my enduring relationships."*

**Spirituality**

*"I gracefully jump over all hurdles in life to build an enduring spirit."*

Activities

## Sports and Games: *Monopoly*
### Key Associations: self-interest, power

*Monopoly* is a game in which the accumulation of wealth is the goal. When playing *Monopoly*, recognize your own right to exercise power in life situations. Acknowledge that your interests are valid and your goals are important if you are to achieve happiness.

**Physical Wellness**

*"I have a right to make my physical body healthy and powerful."*

**Mental Wellness**

*"I am chiefly interested in my own mental welfare."*

**Career and Finances**

*"I work with my own power to accumulate wealth and success."*

**Relationships**

*"I recognize my own power and my own needs in my relationships."*

**Spirituality**

*"I work toward the accumulation of true spiritual wealth."*

Activities

## Sports and Games: Puzzles
### Key Associations: problem solving, self-analysis

Putting a puzzle together (particularly a jigsaw) is an exercise in reasoning and problem solving. It's a wonderful metaphor for analyzing and solving the puzzles of self and circumstance—for fitting the "pieces" together. When working on a puzzle, consider how every puzzling aspect of life has its place in the big picture, so to speak.

**Physical Wellness**

*"I solve the puzzles of the body to achieve physical wholeness."*
*"With patience and intelligence, I become the picture of perfect health."*

**Mental Wellness**

*"I have an amazing mind for problem solving."*
*"I sort and analyze puzzling thoughts and feelings."*

**Career and Finances**

*"I work toward solving the puzzles of my career."*
*"I analyze and solve my financial situation."*

**Relationships**

*"I solve problems in my relationships with patience and intelligence."*
*"I place problems in my relationships in proper perspective."*

**Spirituality**

*"The divine puts the pieces of my life and soul in perfect order."*

Activities

## Sports and Games: Running
### Key Associations: fast movement, effort, stamina, pacing

Running or jogging requires relatively fast movement and, therefore, takes significant effort to build stamina. There are also pacing issues involved. The fast movement is a metaphor for making haste in order to achieve our goals. Effort and ever-increasing constitution are also highly prized to improve the self. And pacing ourselves in life is very important, so we don't burn out or "get winded." When running or jogging, consider how making a strong effort in your life will quickly propel you toward obtaining your self-improvement goals.

**Physical Wellness**

*"I use my full effort to quickly improve my physical health."*

**Mental Wellness**

*"I pace myself as I move rapidly to a healthy and balanced mind."*

**Career and Finances**

*"I build the constitution needed to achieve success as quickly as possible."*
*"I pace myself to make wise decisions for career and financial matters."*

**Relationships**

*"I use effort to build long-lasting and healthy relationships."*

**Spirituality**

*"I build spiritual stamina as I make my way quickly toward spiritual mastery."*

## Sports and Games: Skating
### Key Associations: speed, gracefulness, balance

Skating requires skill in order to be balanced, quick, and graceful. Sayings like "she skates through life" indicate the ideas of ease and grace seen in skaters, but do not take into account the time and effort required to be masterful. When skating, recognize how you are becoming more and more skillful in your life to give you the ability to create balanced changes quickly and gracefully.

**Physical Wellness**
*"I gracefully speed my way to better bodily health."*

**Mental Wellness**
*"I move gracefully and quickly toward greater mental balance and happiness."*

**Career and Finances**
*"I develop skills to move quickly and gracefully toward my career goals."*
*"I master skills to achieve balance in my finances."*

**Relationships**
*"I speak and act with grace and poise in all of my relationships."*

**Spirituality**
*"The divine expresses grace and mastery through my life."*

## Sports and Games: Skiing
### Key Associations: fast and balanced change, joy

Skiing involves maintaining balance at high speeds, which leads to the joy of this activity. This is a metaphor for the ability to rapidly change from one state of mind or experience to another in a balanced and joyful fashion. While skiing, realize the ever-increasing balance in your life that allows you to make self-directed changes quickly.

**Physical Wellness**

*"I move rapidly and joyfully toward a state of total health and wellness."*

**Mental Wellness**

*"I quickly and adeptly direct my thoughts and emotions in joyous directions."*

**Career and Finances**

*"I joyfully speed my way to greater levels of material success."*

**Relationships**

*"I joyfully experience and direct healthy changes in my relationships."*

**Spirituality**

*"I joyfully experience and direct rapid changes in my life on my spiritual journey."*

## Sports and Games: Soccer
### Key Associations: cooperation, achievement

Soccer demands cooperation with other members of the team in order to score goals, thus it contains metaphors for working with multiple aspects of the self (your "team") in order to reach a specific life goal. Because soccer is mostly played with legs and feet, it is a particular symbol for support and directed movement. When you play soccer, recognize that all members of your team represent aspects of your own mind or personality. Realize that there are specific steps you need to take in your life to reach your current improvement goal.

**Physical Wellness**

*"I work with all aspects of mind and body to attain the goal of perfect health."*

**Mental Wellness**

*"I recognize all aspects of my mind and personality as essential for a balanced mind."*

**Career and Finances**

*"I utilize all resources and support to attain my career and financial goals."*
*"I skillfully direct my way to the goal of success."*

**Relationships**

*"I move closer and closer to the goal of healthy and happy relationships."*

**Spirituality**

*"I work with all aspects of mind and soul to attain my spiritual destiny."*

## Sports and Games: Swimming
### Key Associations: emotional mastery

Swimming for fun or sport requires skill and comfort in the water. Water is a symbol for the realm of emotions. Thus, swimming is a metaphor for successfully dealing with our own emotions in our current situation or environment. As you swim, recognize that attaining more mastery over your emotional state can play a huge factor in all areas of life. Think of how life would improve if you could minimize negative emotional states.

**Physical Wellness**

*"I skillfully control the way I feel about my body and my health."*

**Mental Wellness**

*"I master my emotions to live a happy and satisfying life."*
*"I grow more and more comfortable with my feeling nature."*

**Career and Finances**

*"I am in control over my feelings about money."*
*"I skillfully decide how I feel about my career path."*

**Relationships**

*"I gain more and more control over my feelings in my relationships."*
*"I control my moods when I am around others."*

**Spirituality**

*"I develop control in my emotional nature."*

## Sports and Games: Tennis
### Key Associations: self-control, accuracy

Tennis requires a great deal of accuracy and self-control to keep the ball in play. And when people use the tennis metaphor of "acing" this or that, they refer to the skill, control, and accuracy needed to claim victory in some pursuit. In a like manner, self-control and specific actions are often requirements to create positive change. As you play tennis, realize how you are gaining more self-control day by day in order to accurately achieve your goals.

**Physical Wellness**

*"I gain more and more control over my health through accurate planning."*

**Mental Wellness**

*"I develop more self-control over my thoughts and emotions."*
*"I choose accurate beliefs to build high self esteem and confidence."*

**Career and Finances**

*"I have tremendous self-control over my finances."*
*"I skillfully maneuver my career in winning directions."*

**Relationships**

*"I use accurate communication and self-control to develop winning relationships."*

**Spirituality**

*"I develop more self-control to assist myself in spiritual victory."*

---

190

## Sports and Games: Trivia
### Key Associations: memory, knowledge utilization

Trivia games call upon players' knowledge of seemingly unimportant matters in order to win. In a similar way, all of our experiences help us to gain knowledge and wisdom that may be unexpectedly called upon at a later time to help us achieve or improve. When playing a trivia game, it's a reminder that the bits and pieces of knowledge and wisdom gained in daily life can help you reach your goals.

**Physical Wellness**
*"I use all of my knowledge and wisdom to create and maintain my health."*

**Mental Wellness**
*"I know what I need to achieve a balanced mind."*

**Career and Finances**
*"I use all of my knowledge to succeed in my career and financial goals."*

**Relationships**
*"I utilize the knowledge and wisdom I've gained to create and maintain good relationships."*

**Spirituality**
*"All of my knowledge helps me toward spiritual fulfillment."*

Activities

## Sports and Games: Video Games
### Key Associations: overcoming obstacles, persistence

Most video games involve overcoming obstacles (zapping the bad guys) in order to win. Through repeated play, skill levels are achieved to gain mastery. This is a marvelous analogy for overcoming obstacles in life through persistence. Many of our self-improvement goals will manifest if we learn to master the skills we need to achieve them. When playing a video game, recognize the obstacles you need to overcome in order to "win." Realize that with effort and time comes the skill you need to achieve your goal.

**Physical Wellness**
*"I overcome all obstacles to physical health."*
*"I skillfully achieve higher levels of wellness."*

**Mental Wellness**
*"One by one, I remove all mental barriers to happiness and peace."*
*"My mental skills are increasing with time and effort."*

**Career and Finances**
*"I overcome all barriers to financial success."*
*"I gain higher levels of skill and mastery in my career."*

**Relationships**
*"I skillfully overcome obstacles to happy, healthy relationships."*
*"My skills take me to higher and deeper levels in my relationships."*

**Spirituality**
*"I develop the skills I need to achieve my spiritual goals."*
*"I work my way to higher levels of spiritual achievement."*

## Sports and Games: Working Out
### Key Associations: self-effort, process, resolution

Working out is full of symbolism. A common saying is that someone is "working out his problems." This suggests using effort to reach a resolution. Thus working out our bodies to improve our health, strength, or appearance provides a metaphor for all of those issues of life for which we need to apply effort in order to attain our goals. Weight-bearing exercises symbolically remind us that resistance builds strength in all areas of life. When working out, embrace the realization that effort to improve in any area requires patience and commitment in order to reap the benefit.

**Physical Wellness**

*"I use my effort to become stronger, healthier, and more attractive."*

**Mental Wellness**

*"I work out my mental and emotional challenges to create inner peace."*

**Career and Finances**

*"I work out my career and financial challenges to support a comfortable lifestyle."*

**Relationships**

*"I work out the challenges in my relationships."*

**Spirituality**

*"I use my effort to grow spiritually stronger."*

## Sports and Games: Wrestling
### Key Associations: strength, stamina, effort

Wrestling requires and builds tremendous strength and endurance. Thus, this activity is an apt metaphor for the inner strength and stamina that are gained through adversity, which are then used to achieve a goal. When wrestling, recognize how your struggle in an area of development is actually making you a stronger person. Realize that, with effort, you can defeat any obstacle to your success.

**Physical Wellness**

*"I am becoming a stronger person through fighting disease."*
*"I use my effort to become healthy and strong."*

**Mental Wellness**

*"All of my problems are making me mentally stronger."*

**Career and Finances**

*"With effort and endurance, I build a strong career."*

**Relationships**

*n/a*

**Spirituality**

*"The divine gives me challenges to build my spiritual strength."*

## Standing Up
### Key Associations: recognition, self-assertion

Standing up from a seated or reclining position is a metaphor for self-assertion and recognition as revealed by the well-known phrase "stand up for yourself." It carries with it the idea of expressing and valuing one's rights, opinions, and worth, even in the face of possible scorn or derision from others. Of course, sometimes it is our own poor behavior, attitudes, or beliefs we need to stand up to, rather than other people. Whenever you move to a standing position, consider who or what you need to confront in your life. Think of what more courage could do for you in the way of self-improvement.

**Physical Wellness**

*"I take a stand for my health and the well-being of my physical body."*

**Mental Wellness**

*"I stand up and counter any undesirable thoughts my mind generates."*
*"I stand up to my feelings of fear, anger, and resentment."*

**Career and Finances**

*"I stand up to voice my business acumen and ideas."*
*"I stand up to those who deal with me unfairly."*

**Relationships**

*"I stand up for myself in all of my relationships."*
*"I stand up for what I want in my relationships."*

**Spirituality**

*"I stand up for my spiritual principles."*
*"I take a stand in my spiritual beliefs."*

Activities

## Starting the Car
### Key Associations: initiative, power

Starting a car (or any motor vehicle) represents having power, taking personal initiative, or generating energy toward some goal or project. The car itself can represent the physical body, the ego, or any "vehicle" of attainment, such as a business or an investment. The car key represents access to knowledge and potential (the key). Turning on the ignition represents initializing or actualizing that knowledge and power. This is a marvelous metaphor for self-empowerment or for putting effort toward any sort of attainment. Colloquialisms such as "that really turns me on" reveal part of the message of this activity.

**Physical Wellness**

*"I ignite the healthy processes of my body to function perfectly."*

**Mental Wellness**

*"I ignite my mental processes."*

*"I turn on the power of my thoughts and emotions to experience my power."*

**Career and Finances**

*"I initiate the process that leads me toward financial gain."*

*"I start the engine of new ideas for making money."*

**Relationships**

*"I initialize my power to have satisfying relationships."*

*"I restart the engine of my desire to love."*

**Spirituality**

*"I am turned on by spiritual advancement and knowledge."*

## Taking out the Trash
### Key Associations: clearing, releasing, eliminating

Taking out the trash is a symbolic activity for removing from life that which is no longer of any use, of clearing away the "clutter" of our lives. This may include outmoded beliefs, attitudes, or behaviors. As you remove the trash from your home, recognize how important it is to recognize and eliminate things from our lives that were once useful to us but now must be released for keeping the House of Self clean and orderly.

**Physical Wellness**

*"I efficiently eliminate from my body what it no longer uses for good health."*
*"I throw out unhealthy beliefs and attitudes about my body."*

**Mental Wellness**

*"I throw out outworn thoughts, feelings, and beliefs to maintain an orderly mind."*

**Career and Finances**

*"I throw out old, unprofitable ideas that no longer assist my success."*

**Relationships**

*"I throw out immature attitudes and behaviors to make my relationships healthier."*

**Spirituality**

*"I throw out old beliefs and dogma that no longer serve me so my soul can be purer and happier."*

## Touching
### Key Associations: direct contact, experience

To touch anything or anyone is to make direct contact with it. This is a grand metaphor for having or gaining direct experiences that allow us to understand ourselves and our lives in a real and undeniable way. Whenever you touch anything, realize you are simultaneously coming into contact, symbolically, with an aspect of your own being. Recognize the value of true experience in life over mere theory and speculation. You might even consider the significance of the common metaphor "getting your hands dirty."

**Physical Wellness**

*"I experience my physical body and understand its reality and importance."*

**Mental Wellness**

*"I make direct contact with my inner mind and experience its amazing functions and powers."*

**Career and Finances**

*"I make contact with whatever I need to advance my career and grow financially."*

*"I experience what I need in the real world to become wealthy and successful."*

**Relationships**

*"I connect with people in a real and vivid manner."*

*"I make a strong connection with those I really care about."*

**Spirituality**

*"I make contact with the divine and have authentic spiritual experiences."*

*"I recognize the divine creator at work in everything I touch."*

Activities

## Traveling
### Key Associations: change, self-exploration

When we travel, whether near or far and by whatever means, we expose ourselves to new and different places, people, and ways of life. So traveling is a metaphor for expanding, exploring, and changing the self. And the application is universal to self-improvement. When you are traveling, remind yourself that you are changing and are open to that change. Be ready for changes in beliefs, attitudes, and ways of responding to life so you can reach your self-improvement goals.

**Physical Wellness**

*"I am on a journey to better health and increased energy."*

**Mental Wellness**

*"I am on a journey to a sharper, clearer mind and more centered emotions."*

**Career and Finances**

*"I am on a journey to greater success and abundance."*

**Relationships**

*"I am on a journey to explore and expand healthy relationships."*

**Spirituality**

*"I am on a spiritual journey that takes me toward my divine destination."*

## Turning on a Light
### Key Associations: realization, knowledge, energy

Turning on a light is a metaphor for knowledge of self or of circumstances or coming to some realization about life. It's important to recognize that turning on the light is an act of self-volition. In other words, we take the action needed to illuminate our way. This activity reminds us that we have a choice: whether to allow ourselves to see or to remain in darkness. The light won't go on until we choose to "flip the switch." Turning on a light can also symbolize enthusiasm, motivation, or intense interest, as revealed by the saying "that really turns me on." As you turn on a light, consider how more knowledge or energy could improve your life in your target areas.

**Physical Wellness**
*"I light the way to complete physical health."*

**Mental Wellness**
*"I flip the switches of my mind that give me understanding and knowledge."*

**Career and Finances**
*"I turn on the power to new ideas for making money."*
*"I flip the switch that empowers me in my career."*

**Relationships**
*"I am turned on in my relationship."*
*"I am empowered for understanding my relationships with others."*

**Spirituality**
*"I recognize and access divine power and truth."*
*"I am turned on to the divine within."*

## Tying Your Shoes
### Key Associations: binding, details

Shoes protect the feet. Among other things, feet are a symbol of the direction your life is taking. Tying shoes is a means of binding the shoes to the feet. So tying them is a metaphor for taking care of or paying attention to important and obvious details that can impact the choices you make. When you tie your shoes, realize that the details of your plans for change and growth are important factors in your success.

**Physical Wellness**

*"I tie up loose ends, considering all the details that can improve my physical wellness."*

**Mental Wellness**

*"I take care of the details of my mental wellness, leaving no loose ends."*

**Career and Finances**

*"I tie up the loose ends of my financial matters, taking details into consideration."*

*"I prepare for further success in my career by binding up the details."*

**Relationships**

*"I tie up the loose ends of my relationships that they may be harmonious and complete."*

**Spiritual Wellness**

*"I pay attention to the details of my spiritual life that I may proceed on my path."*

## Unlocking a Door
### Key Associations: gaining access

A door is a barrier between two places. Unlocking a door, therefore, is a means of gaining access to another place. Metaphorically, it may be self-knowledge we want access to, or perhaps unrealized potential locked away in the mind, or even a healthier condition of the body. Whenever you unlock any door, recognize that you have access to knowledge and opportunities.

**Physical Wellness**
> *"I unlock the door leading to health and wellness."*
> *"I have access to perfect health."*

**Mental Wellness**
> *"I unlock to door to better ways of thinking and feeling."*

**Career and Finances**
> *"I gain access to greater monetary supply."*
> *"I unlock the door leading to a better career."*

**Relationships**
> *"I unlock the door to my inner self to obtain honest, intimate relationships."*

**Spirituality**
> *"I unlock the door to more spiritual realization and fulfillment."*

Activities

## Unplugging
### Key Associations: discontinuance, detaching

Unplugging an electric appliance of any kind can be used as a metaphor for discontinuing or detaching from beliefs, thoughts, and behaviors that are currently unneeded. Part of learning what we need to do to improve is learning what we need to stop doing, what we need to unplug in our lives. As you pull the plug on an electrical device, recognize your ability to stop making power available to that which no longer serves any useful purpose for you.

**Physical Wellness**

*"I pull the plug on sickness and disease and give it no more potential power."*

*"I detach from unnecessary activities that might use precious power from my body."*

**Mental Wellness**

*"I offer no more power to thoughts and feelings that no longer serve my mind."*

**Career and Wellness**

*"I pull the plug on that which might waste my financial resources."*

**Relationships**

*"I detach from hurtful, harmful relationships and remove their power."*

*"I discontinue negative thoughts and behaviors that take power away from my relationships."*

**Spirituality**

*"I detach myself from any belief or behavior that is no longer of value in my spiritual development."*

Activities

## Using the Toilet
### Key Associations: release, elimination

Just as we need to rid our bodies of waste and toxins, so too do we need to get rid of unusable mental and emotional waste from our minds. The acts of urinating and defecation on a symbolic level have to do with the concept of elimination or release of that which is no longer of use. urinating can be symbolic for releasing negative or immature feelings and thoughts. Defecation can be used as a clear metaphor for eliminating undesirable patterns of behavior or letting go of the past.

**Physical Wellness**
*"I eliminate all undesirable conditions of the body and return to perfect health."*
*"I release from my body that which it cannot use."*
*"I flush away all physical and mental toxicity and waste."*

**Mental Wellness**
*"I eliminate anger, fear, and resentment from my life."*
*"I let go of wasteful thoughts, beliefs, and behaviors."*
*"I relieve myself of the past"*

**Career and Finances**
*"I eliminate wasteful spending from my behavior."*
*"I let go of undesirable thoughts and feelings about money."*
*"I flush away impoverished thinking and feelings."*

**Relationships**
*"I let go of negative thoughts and feelings about others in my life."*
*"I release myself from immature ways of treating those whom I love."*
*"I eliminate feelings of anger and resentment about people in my life."*

**Spirituality**
*"I rid myself of old patterns of thought and emotion that no longer serve me."*
*"I let go of immature ways of thinking, feeling, and doing."*
*"I eliminate from my life activities that keep me from advancing my relationship with the divine."*

Activities

## Vacuuming
### Key Associations: clearing foundation

Vacuuming a carpet or floor is symbolic for clearing and maintaining the foundations of life. This could apply to the foundation of physical or mental health, the foundation of love in relationships, etc. The suctioning action contains a powerful image and metaphor with the "lifting away" of accumulated debris. As you vacuum, consider what undesirable accumulated thoughts, behaviors, and beliefs need to be lifted away from your life.

**Physical Wellness**

*"I clear away unhealthy thoughts and behaviors that interfere with the foundation of my physical health."*

**Mental Wellness**

*"I remove the accumulated debris of negative thoughts to maintain the foundation of a healthy mind."*

**Career and Finances**

*"I clear away accumulated habits that keep me from a strong financial foundation."*

**Relationships**

*"I remove from my behavior and attitude that which interferes with the foundation of my relationships."*

**Spirituality**

*"I clear away the debris of negativity from my spiritual foundation."*

# Waiting
## Key Associations: process, expectation, destiny

We wait for things with the expectation that we will arrive somewhere, receive something, or achieve something in due time. Therefore, waiting is symbolic for the anticipation of victory, triumph, or merely the manifestation of some desired thing or condition. For instance, those who wait in a traffic jam recognize that in spite of the delay, they will eventually reach their destination. As another example, we know that when we put a cake in the oven, we must wait until the baking process is finished. Waiting, therefore, should not be seen as a source of aggravation, but rather, as an important part of any process. As you wait for anything, realize how in due time you expect to achieve improvement and success in your target areas.

**Physical Wellness**

*"I expect the natural processes of my body to bring and sustain perfect health."*

**Mental Wellness**

*"I process new experiences and expect to learn from them."*

*"I patiently allow my mind to process thoughts and feelings."*

**Career and Finances**

*"I wait for and recognize opportunities for increased prosperity."*

**Relationships**

*"I anticipate good things from my relationships."*

**Spirituality**

*"My spiritual development is in process."*

*"I anticipate my spiritual growth."*

*"I wait for the divine to illuminate my path."*

Activities

## Walking
### Key Associations: movement, change, self-support

Walking primarily involves the legs and feet in a highly coordinated movement requiring tremendous balance. Walking is, therefore, a metaphor for making self-supported, balanced changes in life. While walking, credit yourself for the grace and poise you possess to direct your life toward your goals.

**Physical Wellness**

*"I support myself with balance and poise to become healthier."*

**Mental Wellness**

*"I move myself with grace toward a peaceful and balanced mind."*

**Career and Finances**

*"I direct and support myself in becoming more successful."*

**Relationships**

*"I make balanced changes in my relationships to support my own needs."*

**Spirituality**

*"I move gracefully toward an ever-greater spirit-centered life."*

# Washing Hands
## Key Associations: release, termination

Washing your hands is a symbol for releasing or terminating any activity or idea that is counterproductive or harmful to your purpose. I've included a separate entry for this form of self-cleansing because it is such a common and powerful activity. Sayings like, "I wash my hands of it" reveal the metaphorical meaning of this activity. As you wash your hands, consider what thoughts you need to eliminate from your mind and what behaviors might contaminate your improvement efforts.

**Physical Wellness**

*"I wash my hands of all that prevents me from achieving optimum physical condition."*

**Mental Wellness**

*"I wash my hands of all contaminated thoughts and attitudes."*

**Career and Finances**

*"I wash my hands of behaviors and beliefs that do not serve my success."*

**Relationships**

*"I wash my hands of harmful relationships."*

*"I wash my hands of any contaminated attitudes and behaviors in my relationships."*

**Spirituality**

*"I wash my hands of all spiritually counterproductive beliefs, attitudes, and behaviors."*

## Watching
### Key Associations: awareness, observation

Watching anyone or anything of interest is a conscious act involving awareness and observation. From watching, we can learn a great deal. Symbolically, we can recognize that we need to be more aware of ourselves, and in so doing, come to understand ourselves in new ways. When you watch anything, recognize what aspect of self the object of your attention may represent. And realize how just turning your attention and awareness to it may change it for the better.

**Physical Wellness**

*"I actively observe my physical body and become more aware of its form and functions."*

**Mental Wellness**

*"I consciously observe my own thinking patterns to understand my own mind better."*

*"My powers of observation are excellent."*

**Career and Finances**

*"I observe with great interest my thoughts and actions regarding my career."*

*"I become aware of the way I react and respond to money."*

*"I develop keen awareness of all financial matters."*

**Relationships**

*"I observe my relationships with others and am aware of my own behaviors and attitudes."*

**Spirituality**

*"I observe myself from a higher perspective and become more self-aware."*

# Working (general)
## Key Associations: effort for reward, service

Work, in general, represents the idea of using personal effort to achieve or obtain a specific reward. And whether we are talking about the body, mind, career, or spirit, effort of some kind is required to improve. Thus, the concept of work has virtually universal applications to remind ourselves of the work of self-improvement. When you are working at your job, recognize your ability to make strides toward your self-improvement goals.

**Physical Wellness**

*"I work toward improving my health and wellness."*

**Mental Wellness**

*"I work for a sharp and balanced mind."*

*"I use my effort to create my own happiness."*

**Career and Finances**

*"I work toward a bright and abundant future."*

*"I earn the rewards of my labor."*

**Relationships**

*"I make an effort and work toward excellent and loving relationships."*

**Spirituality**

*"I work toward enlightenment and realization."*

*"I use effort to reach toward the divine."*

Activities

## Working: Accountant
### Key Associations: attention, inventory, responsibility

Accounting is a metaphor for taking stock of and responsibility for one's life. Just as an accountant takes a detailed inventory and assessment of monetary assets, we can also take such care when it comes to our health, our relationships, and so forth. Accounting is symbolic for paying attention to what accrues in our personal lives. When you approach your job as an accountant, recognize that you are responsible for the assets of your own life and learn how to work with those assets to your greatest advantage.

**Physical Wellness**

*"I take responsibility for the health of my body."*

**Mental Wellness**

*"I pay attention to my thoughts and feelings."*
*"I account for my own mental wellness."*

**Career and Finances**

*"I pay close attention to my career path."*
*"I make a careful account of my own finances."*

**Relationships**

*"I give my relationships the attention they need to flourish."*

**Spirituality**

*"I take account of my relationship with the divine."*
*"I place the details of my spiritual life in order."*

Activities

## Working: Actor
### Key Associations: self-change, adaptability

An actor takes on a role in order to play a part in a show. He or she becomes someone else for a while in order to entertain an audience and then gets paid for it. Similarly, there are many roles we decide to play in life. Our ability to adapt and change ourselves frequently determines the quality of life we experience. When acting, recognize how you are emerging as an adaptable human being. Begin to see the roles you play in real life and how best to play them.

**Physical Wellness**
*"I transmute myself into a healthier human being."*

**Mental Wellness**
*"I am adaptable and changeable while never losing sight of my true self."*

**Career and Finances**
*"I willingly play the role of a successful and wealthy individual."*

**Relationships**
*"I play healthy roles in all of my relationships."*

**Spirituality**
*"I play my part in the divine show of life."*

Activities

## Working: Administrative Assistant
### Key Associations: organization, assistance

Any type of administrative or clerical work offers a metaphor for promoting more order and organization in life and calling upon inner resources (assistance) to advance. As you go about your administrative duties, recognize that you are simultaneously assisting yourself in your goals. See yourself as your own best helper.

**Physical Wellness**

*"I assist my body in producing perfect health."*

**Mental Wellness**

*"I organize my thoughts and feelings to create mental harmony."*

**Career and Finances**

*"I call upon my resources to help me achieve success."*

**Relationships**

*"I administrate loving and lasting relationships."*

**Spirituality**

*"I assist my soul to advance my spiritual walk."*

## Working: Agent
### Key Associations: volition, access, connection

If you are an agent (for example, literary, sports, actor, modeling) you act as a representative and catalyst to help your clients succeed. You are successful because you have access to certain people in the industry. This is symbolic for having access and connections to your own inner mind and powers to further your own success or progress. As you go about your job, consider that you can communicate with that part of you that makes success and positive change happen.

**Physical Wellness**

*"I access and influence my body to have optimum health."*

**Mental Wellness**

*"I access important areas of thought and emotion to promote positive change."*

**Career and Finances**

*"I access my inner drive and ambition to achieve the success I deserve."*

**Relationships**

*"I access my inner resources to change my relationships in positive ways."*

**Spirituality**

*"I access the divine to further my spiritual progress."*

## Working: Architect
### Key Associations: planning, exactitude, measurement

As an architect you develop and provide precise plans that are used to construct buildings. In a similar manner, you are the "architect" of your own life. You can and should create plans that build that kind of structure for your life. As you go about your job, consider what kind of life you are building for yourself. Do you use the same care as you do in planning a building?

**Physical Wellness**

*"I develop exact plans to build a strong, functional, and beautiful body."*

**Mental Wellness**

*"I use great thought and planning to create a strong, balanced mind."*

*"I am the architect of my mind, and I create magnificent structures of thought."*

**Career and Finances**

*"I am the architect of my career."*

*"I develop a specific plan to create strong and flexible finances."*

**Relationships**

*"I develop strong and beautiful relationships carefully and skillfully."*

**Spirituality**

*"I use knowledge to construct a spiritual life."*

## Working: Athlete
### Key Associations: inner strength, skill, attainment

As a professional athlete, you use a combination of physical strength and coordinated movements to succeed in your sport. It is also very likely that you compete with others in order to make your living. It is inner strength and resolve, along with great skill, that are often required to succeed with athletic goals. In the end we find that we are always in competition—not with others necessarily, but with ourselves. We compete against the inner voices of self-doubt and lethargy. When engaged as an athlete, recognize how you can apply your sense of inner determination to defeat negative thoughts regarding your self-improvement goals.

**Physical Wellness**

*"I use all of my inner strength and determination to win the victory of good health."*

**Mental Wellness**

*"I defeat the competition of negative thoughts with happy and uplifting ones."*

*"I call upon my inner strength and skills of thought to attain a balanced mind-set."*

**Career and Finances**

*"I use all of my skill and inner strength to attain success."*

**Relationships**

*"I build strong relationship skills to attain happiness in all of my relationships."*

**Spirituality**

*"The divine expresses through me a strong and highly developed spirit."*

## Working: Automotive Mechanic
### Key Associations: power, self-mastery

As a mechanic, you understand how the parts of an automobile work in tandem with other parts and know what to do to make them work at their most efficient. This is a metaphor for the inner workings of the mind and body. There are also those who work with the frame (or body) of automobiles, which is an apt metaphor for the personality as it is perceived by others or with the external appearance of the physical body. While fixing vehicles, realize your inner power to fix yourself. Recognize that you are gaining more self-knowledge every day.

**Physical Wellness**

*"I maintain and repair my body to work at maximum power and efficiency."*

*"I work on the appearance of my body to express beauty and power."*

**Mental Wellness**

*"I master the mechanisms of my own mind to run smoothly and powerfully."*

*"I express myself to others as powerful and efficient."*

**Career and Finances**

*"I run my financial life like a fine-tuned engine."*

*"I master the mechanics of my finances to get the most from them."*

**Relationships**

*"I master the mechanics of a well-maintained relationship."*

**Spirituality**

*"I work with my spiritual tools to gain self-mastery."*

## Working: Banker
### Key Associations: wealth, reliability, preservation

A bank is a place to keep wealth in order to preserve or compound it. The colloquialism "you can bank on that" underscores its association with trust and reliability. Thus, activities of the banker are metaphors for dealing with trustworthiness and preservation of the "wealth" of life, such as health of body, mind, or relationships.

**Physical Wellness**
*"I take care of the wealth of my physical body."*
*"I preserve and add to the wellness of my body."*

**Mental Wellness**
*"I protect and preserve the wealth of my sound mind."*

**Career and Finances**
*"I protect and accrue great material wealth."*

**Relationships**
*"I value and preserve the wealth of my relationships."*

**Spirituality**
*"I bank on my spiritual values."*
*"I manage and protect my wealthy spirit."*

## Working: Broadcaster
### Key Associations: communication, expression

Broadcasting is a means of communicating with others. A job in the broadcasting field is symbolic for the quality and accuracy of communication with others or with multiple aspects of self. How and what we say to others and to ourselves will largely determine the quality of our experiences. For instance, what messages are we inadvertently broadcasting to the cells of our own bodies and how does this affect their functioning? If the job is that of on-air talent, the meaning has to do with the outer presentation of information. If the job is production oriented, analogies around the intentions and processing of our communication may be drawn. If the job is a technical one, it can be a symbol for our specific skills regarding self-expression.

**Physical Wellness**

*"I broadcast messages of life and wellness to my body."*

**Mental Wellness**

*"I communicate honestly and accurately with all levels of my mind."*

*"I broadcast love and encouragement to my inner mind."*

**Career and Finances**

*"I express myself with poise and professionalism."*

**Relationships**

*"I broadcast love and respect to my family, friends, and loved ones."*

**Spirituality**

*"I am a center of expression for the divine will."*

Activities

## Working: Business Developer
### Key Associations: self-development, details

A business is a metaphor for the self in all of its complexity. The business developer, therefore, is a wonderful symbol for the development of the self though attention to practical plans and details. When engaged in this job, consider that you are developing a life plan in order to improve yourself. Realize that creating success for yourself is similar to the way you create success for businesses.

**Physical Wellness**

*"I develop the business of a well-working body."*

**Mental Wellness**

*"I take practical steps to develop my mind and creativity."*

**Career and Finances**

*"I develop my career and financial future with careful attention."*

**Relationships**

*"I develop my relationships with care and success."*

**Spirituality**

*"I develop my spiritual life through practical steps."*

Activities

## Working: Computer Programmer
### Key Associations: process, change

Computer programming is a metaphor for taking an active role in the way we process information and for manifesting change in our lives. It's an analogy for programming ourselves for success, health, and productivity.

**Physical Wellness**

*"I program my mind for a strong, healthy, and attractive body."*

**Mental Wellness**

*"I program my mind to produce clear and balanced thoughts."*

**Career and Finances**

*"I program my mind to achieve successful outcomes in career and finances."*

**Relationships**

*n/a*

**Spirituality**

*"I program my mind to adhere to my spiritual principles."*

## Working: Construction Worker
### Key Associations: creation, building

The activities involved in construction work are symbolic for the building or creation of aspects of the self. Truly we construct our lives with the physical, mental, emotional, and spiritual resources we have, using skills and tools of consciousness with which we have proficiency or mastery. As you go about construction work, realize that you are the crafter of your own life and you can create beautiful and strong structures of thought to have the best possible life experiences.

**Physical Wellness**

*"I build my body to be strong and healthy "*

**Mental Wellness**

*"I craft healthy structures of thought."*
*"I build my self-confidence with precision and purpose."*

**Career and Finances**

*"I create and build strong financial structures."*
*"I construct my career to match my goals."*

**Relationships**

*"I use tools of communication to build solid relationships."*

**Spirituality**

*"I use tools of consciousness to build a solid spiritual foundation."*

## Working: Consultant
### Key Associations: self-counsel, self-knowledge

When you are a consultant, others seek out your knowledge and advice. The underlying message to yourself is that you possess an innate source of wisdom and knowledge. As you go about your job of consultation, remember that you have access to great wells of knowledge and wisdom about your own life and circumstances from which to draw. And by tapping that resource of inner self, you can guide yourself to better health, improved finances or relationships, and more.

**Physical Wellness**

*"I learn and understand what my body requires for total wellness."*
*"I draw on my inner counsel to have complete health."*

**Mental Wellness**

*"I tap my inner resources to be happy and mentally balanced."*

**Career and Finances**

*"I consult myself about what is best for my finances and career."*

**Relationships**

*"I trust my inner wisdom to produce healthy and beneficial relationships."*

**Spirituality**

*"I listen to my inner voice to guide me on my spiritual journey."*

# Working: Customer Service
## Key Associations: satisfaction, empowerment

If you are in customer service, you provide a means for others to be served and satisfied. The service and satisfaction comes as a result of your access to knowledge and power to change or make something happen. As you go about the activity of customer service, bring to mind that you have access to knowledge and power to serve your own needs and desires. Think of your customers as metaphors for parts of your self that need attention or require change.

**Physical Wellness**

*"I serve my physical body by supplying it with what it requires."*

**Mental Wellness**

*"I am empowered to satisfy my mental and emotional needs."*

**Career and Finances**

*"I access all of my resources to meet my financial and career goals."*

**Relationships**

*"I am knowledgeable and empowered to draw and maintain good relationships."*

**Spirituality**

*"I am in the service of spirit and will satisfy the needs of my soul."*

## Working: Designer
### Key Associations: creation, beautification

Whether you design clothes, interiors, or anything else, you are involved in creating and beautifying something. As you design for others, recognize the ongoing task of creating and beautifying your life and self, of placing things in a pleasing and practical order or of creating something original and dynamic. Your particular area of design will reveal much about how you create and pattern your life.

**Physical Wellness**

*"I beautify my body in order to be healthy and attractive."*

**Mental Wellness**

*"I create wonderful and pleasing patterns of thought."*

**Career and Finances**

*"I design my career and finances to serve and reflect my desires."*

**Relationships**

*"I design my relationships to be dynamic, harmonious, and practical."*

**Spirituality**

*"My soul expresses patterns of beauty."*

## Working: Distribution/Shipping
### Key Associations: giving, receiving

Being involved in the distribution, shipping, and receiving aspects of a business is a metaphor for using your efforts to deliver what you want and need in life to be complete.

**Physical Wellness**

*"I distribute to my body what it needs to be healthy."*

**Mental Wellness**

*"I distribute to my mind the thoughts it needs to be happy and balanced."*

**Career and Finances**

*"I distribute to myself ideas that make me happy and successful."*

**Relationships**

*n/a*

**Spirituality**

*"I distribute to my soul what it requires to be happy and healthy."*

## Working: Educator
### Key Associations: self-knowledge

As an educator, it is your job to provide others with knowledge and how to apply it. This is a symbol for the inner teacher, the part of you that is teaching you the lessons of life through experience. You are both your own teacher and your own student. So as you go about this noble profession, realize that you are in the midst of teaching yourself many things on deeper levels so you may succeed with your self-improvement goals.

**Physical Wellness**

*"I teach myself what I need to know to have a healthy, attractive body."*

**Mental Wellness**

*"I teach myself what I need to learn for a strong, sound mind."*

**Career and Finances**

*"I teach myself what I want to know in order to be successful."*

**Relationships**

*"I teach myself about how to have wonderful and healthy relationships."*

**Spirituality**

*"I teach myself about the things of spirit in my daily life."*

## Working: Engineer
### Key Associations: formulation, creation

An engineer uses knowledge and exact mathematics to construct things. By the same token, you are using your knowledge to construct the life you want. When going about your profession, consider that you are the engineer of your own life and destiny.

**Physical Wellness**

*"I use exact knowledge to construct a strong and healthy body."*

**Mental Wellness**

*"I use great thought and planning to create a strong, balanced mind."*

**Career and Finances**

*"I use my knowledge to engineer my career and finances."*

**Relationships**

*"I use great thoughts to construct healthy and beneficial relationships."*

**Spirituality**

*"I use knowledge to construct a spiritual life."*

36

## Working: Entertainer
## Key Associations: self-communication, self-love

Entertaining is associated with self-expression, and symbolic for self-communication and self-love. As you entertain, consider what you are trying to express in life and to yourself. Pay attention to your needs and desires.

**Physical Wellness**

*"I pay attention to the expressions and communications of my body."*

**Mental Wellness**

*"I express self-love to all aspects of my mind and personality."*

**Career and Finances**

*n/a*

**Relationships**

*"I express the love I have for myself in the way I treat others."*

**Spirituality**

*"I express and communicate divine love and truth."*

Activities

## Working: Executive
### Key Associations: willpower, decisiveness

An executive, generally speaking, makes decisions in order to help run a business or corporation. The will of the executive controls the work of other employees. Symbolically speaking, this job is all about using the will in decisive ways to change or control one's own behavior. When on the job, realize that you are in control over what you do. You have the power to make changes in any and all areas of your life through the utilization of your willpower.

**Physical Wellness**
*"I direct my resources to establish and maintain a healthy and attractive body."*

**Mental Wellness**
*"I direct my thoughts to work toward strong self-esteem and a balanced outlook."*

**Career and Finances**
*"I direct my mind to work toward a healthy financial future."*

**Relationships**
*"I direct my own behavior so I can enjoy loving and healthy relationships."*

**Spirituality**
*"I direct my will to align with the divine."*

## Working: Fire and Rescue
### Key Associations: problem solving, self-empowerment

Putting out fires with water is a metaphor for the dissolution of self-destructive thoughts, activities, or tendencies. And if you are involved with rescuing others, there is a symbol of self-rescue to be considered. As you are called to action in fire and rescue, recognize your abilities to heroically resolve the problems in your life with your skills, intelligence, and sheer courage. Realize that you are your own hero, your own rescuer.

**Physical Wellness**

*"I resolve my health issues with courage and action."*

**Mental Wellness**

*"I recognize my own power to overcome all mental challenges."*
*"I put out the fires of self-destructive thoughts."*
*"I rescue my inner self from negativity and discouragement."*

**Career and Wellness**

*"I courageously resolve financial challenges."*

**Relationships**

*"I rescue myself from harmful relationships."*

**Spirituality**

*"The divine rescues and empowers me."*

## Working: General Labor
### Key Associations: effort, action

Labor jobs of any kind involve direct effort and action. While your occupation may involve plenty of thinking, it nonetheless is all about doing. So labor jobs are a marvelous metaphor for taking action and doing something about our challenges, rather than just thinking or talking about them. When you go about your job, recognize that getting what you want from life is often a result of taking a very "hands-on" approach.

**Physical Wellness**
  *"I take direct action and offer full effort to have a healthy and attractive body."*

**Mental Wellness**
  *"I take action to create a happy and harmonious mind-set."*
  *"I supply consistent effort to have a sharp and disciplined mind."*

**Career and Finances**
  *"I take a hands-on approach to my career and finances."*
  *"I take direct action to accomplish my goals for success."*

**Relationships**
  *"I make an effort to establish and maintain the best possible relationships."*

**Spirituality**
  *"I take direct action to strengthen my relationship with the spiritual."*

Activities

## Working: Government Worker
### Key Associations: self-regulation

If you hold a government job, you help to establish and maintain regulations and programs that make the lives of citizens of your country, state, or province better. Your participation in the government of others is a metaphor for governing or controlling yourself. As you go about your government work, consider the "rules and regulations" you apply to your own life to make it better. Also consider which personal rules may require change to lead you to self-improvement.

**Physical Wellness**

*"I govern the state of my physical body toward greater health and wellness."*

**Mental Wellness**

*"I govern my thoughts and emotions in ways that make me happy and centered."*

**Career and Finances**

*"I govern my finances and career path to become more successful and wealthy."*

**Relationships**

*"I govern my behavior and attitudes to have happy, healthy relationships."*

**Spirituality**

*"I govern my spiritual life to take me closer and closer to my divine goals."*

## Working: Health Care Provider
### Key Associations: self-healing

Whether you are a doctor, nurse, or involved in any capacity with health care, you take part in helping others to heal. So many of our life challenges are a result of mental and emotional "wounds" or "diseases" we accrue. Your health care job offers a metaphor for healing yourself, for restoring your mind and body to a condition of wholeness. When going about your job, consider that you are in the midst of healing that part of you that needs attention.

**Physical Wellness**
*"I help my body repair itself to its natural state of total health."*

**Mental Wellness**
*"I care about my mind and restore it to a state of balance and peace."*

**Career and Finances**
*"I heal my financial situation and restore it to perfect working order."*
*"I care about and maintain my career in good condition."*

**Relationships**
*"I recover from past hurts and restore my relationships to perfect health."*

**Spirituality**
*"I assist my soul to return to a state of pure joy and wholeness."*

## Working: Hotel/Hospitality Worker
### Key Associations: transitions, self-accommodation

Being in the hotel/hospitality business means you help provide accommodations for other people. Hotels in general are a symbol for transitional stages and states of life, mind, or body. So being in the hospitality business is a metaphor for providing yourself what you need in order to make changes in your life. As you go about your hospitality job, recognize that you are capable of giving yourself the support you need as you make changes for self-improvement.

**Physical Wellness**

*"I support myself and provide what I need to improve my body and health."*

**Mental Wellness**

*"I support myself mentally and emotionally."*

**Career and Finances**

*"I support myself as I improve my financial and career situation."*

**Relationships**

*"I support myself in improving my relationships."*

**Spirituality**

*"I support myself as I am in the process of spiritual change."*

## Working: Human Resources
### Key Associations: self-awareness, inner resources

Working in human resources is symbolic for the proper identification and utilization of your personality and abilities. As you deal with placing people in jobs, realize what aspects of your inner self are needed at this time to help your situation.

**Physical Wellness**

*"I identify and employ my resources to improve my body and health."*

**Mental Wellness**

*"I identify and employ my own resources to improve my mental wellness."*

**Career and Finances**

*"I identify and use my inner resources to improve my career and finances."*

**Relationships**

*"I identify my inner resources for developing healthy, harmonious relationships."*

**Spirituality**

*"I identify and utilize my inner spiritual resources."*

Activities

## Working: Installation/Maintenance/Repair
### Key Associations: self-maintenance, self-repair

If you install, maintain, or repair equipment of any kind, your work is a perfect metaphor for "installing" changes for self-improvement, for "maintaining" your current condition, or for "repairing" what needs work in your life. When going about your job, realize that you have the power to change, maintain, and repair yourself using the knowledge and tools available to you.

**Physical Wellness**

*"I install new behaviors into my life for optimum health and fitness."*
*"I maintain my health to function perfectly."*
*"I utilize the knowledge and tools needed to repair my body."*

**Mental Wellness**

*"I install new ways of thinking and feeling to enjoy a happy, balanced mind."*
*"I maintain my sharp and balanced mind with constructive thoughts and attitudes."*
*"I restore balanced and clear thinking with effective knowledge and tools."*

**Career and Finances**

*"I install new plans to supply greater success."*
*"I maintain my finances and career with skill and knowledge."*
*"I repair my career and finances to run at their optimum."*

**Relationships**

*"I implement new strategies to enjoy satisfying relationships."*
*"I maintain my relationships with care and attention."*
*"I repair my relationships with care and attention."*

**Spirituality**

*"I install new spiritual practices that further my spiritual progress."*
*"I maintain my spirit with regular attention and consideration."*
*"I repair my soul with the knowledge and tools I've been given."*

Activities

## Working: Insurance Agent/Worker
### Key Associations: security, precaution

In the insurance industry, you provide security to the customers you serve. This is a symbolic expression for taking action with knowledge and forethought to secure your self-improvement goals. It is also the ability to assess risk. When engaged in your job, think of what steps and precautions you might take to secure your health, your finances, or your relationships. Consider the risks of any new venture.

**Physical Wellness**

*"I take needed steps to secure excellent physical health."*

*"I evaluate the risks of my behavior in regards to my physical health."*

**Mental Wellness**

*"I take needed steps to secure a balanced and clear-thinking mind."*

*"I assess the risks of my thought patterns to my peace of mind."*

**Career and Finances**

*"I use intelligence and forethought to secure the best financial future."*

*"I use intelligence and forethought to secure a satisfying career."*

*"I evaluate the risks of any new financial or career venture."*

**Relationships**

*"I take required action to secure happy, healthy relationships."*

**Spirituality**

*"I use forethought and wisdom to secure my spiritual progress."*

## Working: Inventory
### Key Associations: self-assessment, self-awareness

Taking inventory means assessing and organizing the quantity and quality of a said commodity. This is a metaphor for introspection—for properly assessing, for example, your own behavior, attitudes, and knowledge in relation to your current goals. When taking inventory, realize how "taking stock" and being honest in self-assessment is a vital component to getting where you want to go in life.

**Physical Wellness**

*"I take stock of my health and well-being."*

**Mental Wellness**

*"I am aware of and assess my thoughts, beliefs, and attitudes."*

**Career and Finances**

*"I take inventory of my finances and career."*

**Relationships**

*"I assess my behavior and attitudes toward those I care about."*

**Spirituality**

*"I am aware of my spiritual assets."*

## Working: Law Enforcer
### Key Associations: self-discipline, self-protection

Law enforcement jobs (for example, police or judges) are a metaphor for the discipline needed to protect the self.

**Physical Wellness**

*"I obey the rules of the body to protect and serve its health and well-being."*

**Mental Wellness**

*"I protect and serve my mind and protect it from undesirable thoughts."*

**Career and Finances**

*"I discipline myself to protect my career and finances from harm."*

**Relationships**

*"I regulate my actions and words to protect my relationships from harm."*

**Spirituality**

*"I protect my soul from all harmful influences."*

## Working: Legal/Lawyer
### Key Associations: balance, conflict resolution

Whether you're an attorney, a judge, or involved in other ways in the legal profession, yours is a job of seeking resolution to conflict and balancing what is unjust. This is symbolic for attempting to resolve inner conflicts that interfere with our plans, hopes, and dreams. And the entire justice arena can be seen as a metaphor for seeking to balance areas of life that need it. When involved in your legal profession, consider that you are symbolically balancing and resolving areas of self that are at issue.

**Physical Wellness**

*"I resolve my physical challenges and restore balance to my body."*

**Mental Wellness**

*"I resolve my mental and emotional conflicts and restore my mind to order."*

**Career and Finances**

*"I resolve any internal conflicts with money or my career."*

**Relationships**

*"I resolve problems in my relationships and seek fairness."*

**Spirituality**

*"I resolve that which conflicts with my spiritual beliefs and balance my soul."*

## Working: Mail Carrier
### Key Associations: self-communication

Delivering mail is a metaphor for sending to the inner mind messages you want it to receive. As you do your job, consider what messages you want to get through to your subconscious.

**Physical Wellness**

*"I deliver messages to my inner mind to establish and maintain a healthy body."*

**Mental Wellness**

*"I deliver to my inner mind uplifting and healthy thoughts."*

**Career and Finances**

*"I deliver to my inner mind thoughts that establish and maintain my success."*

**Relationships**

*"I deliver to my inner mind thoughts to help me create and sustain healthy, happy relationships."*

**Spirituality**

*"I deliver to my inner mind messages of hope, peace, and divine love."*

Activities

## Working: Management
### Key Associations: self-management

Managing others in a professional capacity is a metaphor for managing or handling your own life and affairs. As you go about your management position, realize you are in control of your life and the direction you want it to take. Begin to consider how you might manage certain thoughts and behaviors in order to achieve your self-improvement goals.

**Physical Wellness**

*"I manage the condition of my body to produce greater health."*

**Mental Wellness**

*"I successfully manage my mind, thoughts, and emotions."*

**Career and Finances**

*"I manage my career and finances toward greater success."*

**Relationships**

*"I manage my behavior in my relationships to make them better and stronger."*

**Spirituality**

*"I successfully manage my spiritual life to bring myself meaning and fulfillment."*

## Working: Manufacturer
### Key Associations: creating, building

To be involved in the manufacturing of products is to take part in the creation process. In a similar way, you are also in the process of creating your own life, of building new structures of thought and activity. As you approach your manufacturing job, realize that you are capable of manufacturing your experiences and circumstances in a way that is fulfilling to you.

**Physical Wellness**

*"I am building a healthy, strong, and attractive body."*

**Mental Wellness**

*"I manufacture uplifting structures of thought and feeling that produce happiness."*

**Career and Finances**

*"I build my career and finances and enjoy my success."*

**Relationships**

*"I build loving and fulfilling relationships."*

**Spirituality**

*"The divine builds me into the person I am meant to become."*

## Working: Marketer
### Key Associations: presentation, identity

In marketing, you present products to people and give those products recognition and identity. This is symbolic for self-expression and self-recognition. As you do your marketing job, consider how you come across to yourself. What gives you a sense of identity and how does it relate to your self-improvement goals?

**Physical Wellness**

*"I express and identify myself as a healthy, attractive individual."*

**Mental Wellness**

*"I express and identify myself as an interesting, well-balanced personality."*

**Career and Finances**

*"I express and identify myself as successful and wealthy."*

**Relationships**

*"I express and identify myself as a wonderful friend/mate."*

**Spirituality**

*"I express and identify myself as a spiritual person."*

## Working: Nurse
### Key Associations: self-care, compassion

As a nurse, you provide care and compassion to your patients. This is a metaphor for offering necessary care and compassion to heal or to improve you in some way. As you go about your nursing duties, think of ways you can provide care for yourself to get what you most need from your life. Consider whether you are compassionate with yourself about your needs and so-called shortcomings.

**Physical Wellness**

*"I provide compassionate, healing care for my own body."*

**Mental Wellness**

*"I compassionately care for my mind so it restores and maintains balance."*

**Career and Finances**

*"I give care to my finances and career that they may become perfectly healthy."*

**Relationships**

*"I provide compassionate care to my relationships so they may be healthy."*

**Spirituality**

*"I provide loving care to my spirit that it may be healthy and flourish."*

If you are involved in the pharmaceutical industry, you are in the business of providing medicine to help others heal in body and mind. This is symbolic for helping yourself to heal and feel better through your own efforts. As you go about your job, recognize your ability to help areas of your life to greater levels of vitality.

**Physical Wellness**

*"I recognize my own ability to help my body heal and become stronger."*

**Mental Wellness**

*"I help my own mind become stronger and healthier."*

**Career and Finances**

*"I take action to help my finances become strong and healthy."*
*"I take action to help my career flourish."*

**Relationships**

*"I heal myself of past hurts so I can have healthy relationships now."*

**Spirituality**

*"The divine self heals my soul and strengthens my spirit."*

## Working: Professional Services
### Key Associations: self-reliance, self-help

Whatever service you provide, you are in the business of doing for others something that is difficult or inconvenient for them to do for themselves. This is a metaphor for relying on and helping yourself. As you go about your professional service, realize that you are becoming more and more self-reliant in your life and are capable of serving yourself that which you need to be successful and happy.

**Physical Wellness**

*"I realize my capability to help myself attain a state of greater health."*

**Mental Wellness**

*"I help myself satisfy all of my mental and emotional needs."*

**Career and Finances**

*"I recognize how to help myself achieve success in my career and finances."*

**Relationships**

*"I call upon my own abilities and wisdom to establish healthy relationships."*

**Spirituality**

*"I rely on and help myself to attain higher levels of spiritual wisdom."*

Activities

In the publishing field, you not only disseminate information, but you also discriminate (edit) what information is released. This is a metaphor for how you communicate with yourself and with others, and this includes the idea of editing or discarding communications that might be harmful, unprofitable, or counterproductive.

### Physical Wellness
*"I communicate wisely with my body, and I edit unhealthy thoughts and behaviors."*

### Mental Wellness
*"I communicate support and balanced thoughts to my inner mind, and I edit those that are unsupportive or unproductive."*

### Career and Finances
*"I express to myself and others a successful attitude and edit self-doubt and impoverished thinking."*

### Relationships
*"I express love and friendship in my close relationships, and I edit unkind words."*

### Spirituality
*"I express and reflect divine love and edit thoughts and behaviors that are spiritually immature."*

## Working: Quality Control
### Key Associations: quality of life

Quality control as a job is a rather direct analogy for controlling your quality of life. As you go about your profession, realize that you are in charge of controlling the quality of your health, your mind, and your relationships.

**Physical Wellness**

*"I control the quality and condition of my body and its health."*

**Mental Wellness**

*"I control the quality of my thinking and the condition of my mind."*

**Career and Finances**

*"I control my finances and the quality of my career."*

**Relationships**

*"I control the quality of relationships I have with other people."*

**Spirituality**

*"I control the quality of my spiritual life."*

## Working: Researcher
### Key Associations: self-discovery

Research, scientific or otherwise, is a metaphor for seeking self-knowledge. It's all about self-discovery. The kind of research you do may provide even more specific metaphors.

**Physical Wellness**

*"I seek knowledge about my body and health."*

**Mental Wellness**

*"I gain knowledge and discover more about my mind and personality."*

**Career and Finances**

*"I seek knowledge that helps me to discover ways to improve my career and finances."*

**Relationships**

*"I seek knowledge about myself that I may have the best possible relationships."*

**Spirituality**

*"I seek spiritual knowledge and a deeper understanding of who I am."*

## Working: Restaurant/Food Service Worker
### Key Associations: self-service

Providing food for others is a metaphor for providing yourself with what is enjoyable, essential, and sustaining in life. As you prepare or serve food to others, consider what you can do to serve yourself the best of everything possible in life.

**Physical Wellness**

*"I serve my body what it wants and needs for perfect health."*

**Mental Wellness**

*"I serve my mind empowering sources of thought to sustain a healthy mind."*

**Career and Finances**

*"I serve my appetite for an enjoyable career and healthy finances."*

**Relationships**

*"I serve my need for quality relationships."*

**Spirituality**

*"I serve my soul the knowledge and wisdom it needs to be happy and healthy."*

## Working: Salesperson
### Key Associations: self-value

As a salesperson, you help potential buyers recognize the value of products or services. This can be viewed as a metaphor for recognizing or "selling yourself" regarding your own qualities and value. As you go about your sales job, recognize that you possess amazing attributes and qualities that make you a worthwhile human being on this planet. Talk yourself into believing in who you are and what you want.

**Physical Wellness**

*"I am sold on the value of my bodily health and fitness."*

**Mental Wellness**

*"I am sold on my true worth and the qualities I possess."*

**Career and Finances**

*"I am sold on my ability to have more money."*

*"I am sold on my ability to have a better career."*

**Relationships**

*"I am sold on the value of quality relationships."*

**Spirituality**

*"I am sold on the value of a strong spiritual life."*

Activities

---

**261**

## Working: Telecommunications
### Key Associations: self-communication

The field of telecommunications offers a metaphor for communicating with the self on all levels of consciousness. For just as you help provide a service so others can communicate efficiently, the communication you have with your inner self has a strong impact on your quality of life. When approaching your job in telecommunications, realize that you are in constant communication with your mind and even with your body. Consider what messages you want to send and how to send them more effectively.

### Physical Wellness
*"I communicate messages of health and vitality effectively to my body."*

### Mental Wellness
*"I communicate effectively with my own mind to be productive and balanced in my thinking processes."*

### Career and Finances
*"I communicate effective messages of success to my inner self."*

### Relationships
*n/a*

### Spirituality
*"I communicate with all levels of mind and soul."*

Activities

## Working: Therapist
### Key Associations: self-healing, self-talk

The therapist is in the business of helping others to heal. This is a metaphor for all that has to do with self-healing. And therapies of the mind (psychology, hypnotherapy, social work), which use words and ideas to promote change or healing, are marvelous metaphors for positive self-change and self-talk. When engaged in therapy for others, see your clients/patients as general reflections of your own inner self.

**Physical Wellness**

*"I realize my ability to help heal my body."*

**Mental Wellness**

*"I recognize my ability to help my mind heal from all pain."*

**Career and Finances**

*"I recognize my ability to restore my finances and career."*

**Relationships**

*"I recognize my ability to help heal my relationships."*

**Spirituality**

*"I recognize my ability to help heal my own soul."*

## Working: Trainer
### Key Associations: self-empowerment, self-teaching

As any kind of trainer, you essentially empower, teach, and coach others to achieve competence, excellence, or improvement. This is a metaphor for empowering and preparing yourself to meet life challenges and to promote change. When training, consider that you are "in training" for improving your life and circumstances.

**Physical Wellness**

*"I train myself to become healthier, fitter, and more attractive."*

**Mental Wellness**

*"I train my mind to be orderly, efficient, and empowered."*

**Career and Finances**

*"I train myself to become empowered in my career and finances."*

**Relationships**

*"I train myself to create and maintain empowering relationships."*

**Spirituality**

*"I train myself in spiritual disciplines to advance my growth."*

## Working: Transportation
### Key Associations: self-change, self-direction

Being involved in transportation, you help others get from one place to another. This is a metaphor for changing from one state of mind or body to another. You help "transport" your life to where you want it to be. As you go about your transportation duties, consider how you direct your own life and circumstances.

**Physical Wellness**

*"I help my body move to a condition of strength and health."*

**Mental Wellness**

*"I help transport my mind to a place of confident, positive, and healthy thoughts."*

**Career and Finances**

*"I move and direct my career and finances to support my desires and needs."*

**Relationships**

*"I move and direct my thoughts and actions in relationship to others."*

**Spirituality**

*"I transport my soul to higher and better vistas of truth and beauty."*

## Working: Warehouse Worker
### Key Associations: inner and outer resources

A warehouse is a place where resources are stored. If you work in a warehouse, this is a symbol for accessing resources, both internal and external, to produce what you want in your life. As you go about your job, meditate on the idea that everything you need to change your life is at your disposal.

**Physical Wellness**

*"I recognize the resources I need to establish and maintain perfect health."*

**Mental Wellness**

*"I realize the resources I possess to have a sharp and balanced mind."*

**Career and Finances**

*"I recognize all of the resources I have to create abundant wealth and success."*

**Relationships**

*"I recognize the amazing resources I have in my relationships."*

**Spirituality**

*"I recognize that the divine has provided all the resources I need for spiritual progress."*

# 7

## More about Self-Hypnosis Revolution and Changing Your Life

This chapter covers some odds and ends about the method and programs found throughout the book. It also answers some common questions regarding the Self-Hypnosis Revolution process.

### Unlisted Activities

Clearly, I did not include every possible activity in the Compendium. To do so would be exhausting, if not impossible. There may be, therefore, activities in your daily life that are not listed, and you may wonder if those activities can be used in your programs. The answer is an unequivocal yes! A review of Chapter 3 will take you through the process, but below is a summary of how to discover and implement just about any activity into your program:

1. Choose an activity in which you engage with some regularity. The more often you do it in a given day or week, the better.
2. Contemplate and identify the basic associations of the activity. There's no reason to get fancy. Just think about the activity, and off the top of your head consider what associations you might have with it. Then consider whether those associations might metaphorically hold significance for your self-improvement goal.
3. Formulate a beneficial self-suggestion to accompany the activity. Use the associations you made with the activity to formulate simple and direct suggestions pertaining to your target area. Make the suggestions brief and uplifting (see next page).

## Writing Your Own Self-Suggestions

You can write your own self-suggestions to either accommodate an unlisted activity or to take the place of the ones I offer. In fact, I highly recommend that you do so. The very act of concentrating your attention to compose your own suggestions will make a marvelous impression on your subconscious. And in the end, that's really what this whole method is about.

It is true that as a clinical hypnotherapist I have a lot of practice composing suggestions and therefore I may have a leg up on writing pertinent self-suggestions for this method. But there is nothing particularly magical or complicated about the self-suggestions you find in this book. I purposely wrote them in a very straightforward fashion, simply tailoring them to fit the symbolic value of a given activity and to apply to the appropriate target area. You can learn how to write effective self-suggestions by analyzing the structure of the self-suggestions I penned in the Compendium or the ready-to-go programs. My primary recommendation for writing a self-suggestion is that you keep it short and sweet. Long and complicated suggestions are unnecessary because the power of this method is so dramatically augmented by the accompanying activities.

## Frequently Asked Questions

1. *May I add more than the suggested number of activities to my program?* On the planners, there is only room on a template for six activities. The limitation is designed to keep the program from becoming overwhelming. While the initial zeal to incorporate dozens of activities into your program may be genuine, after a few days you would find it taxing. Therefore, I recommend you hold to the prescribed number of activities. If there are more activities you would like to see used in a program, you can always create a new program to use after you complete the current one. In fact, this is highly recommended so you don't get bored with your previous programs. Feeling bored or burdened is

counterproductive to this or any other method of self-improvement.

2. *Do I need to perform activities from my planner in the order in which they are listed?* No. The activities are numbered just to keep track of the total. They are not, nor do they need to be, in any specific order. You use each activity in your program as you encounter it naturally throughout your day. And you will naturally perform some activities more often than others in a given day or week. This is to be expected.

3. *What can I do if there is no listing for my job/work?* It would have been very difficult to list every possible job in the Compendium, as there are literally thousands of types of jobs and specialties. So you can either use the general associations and suggestions for the work listing found in the Compendium or you can use the method discussed above to help decipher the key associations of your job and to help you compose your own self-suggestions.

4. *What if I don't notice any change after using my program?* It is true that some areas of life may require more than a week's application to bring about clear and lasting change. It may, in fact, take several weeks of implementation to see big changes. The good news is that after a week you will find the program is very easy to memorize and incorporate into your daily life. And you can be certain that if you do so, results will make themselves apparent. Positive change is inevitable.

5. *What specific results and changes can I expect from using Self-Hypnosis Revolution?* The exact results of Self-Hypnosis Revolution will depend greatly on the needs, personalities, and circumstances of the user. For instance, if you are using the program to improve your physical wellness, you may encounter a change or shift in your physical condition. Or you might suddenly find the wherewithal to exercise where previously you felt apathetic. You might discover yourself eating more nutritious foods or letting go of some poor dietary habits. The possible changes are many. If you are so inclined, I recommend using a journal to track your results.

6. *Do I have to memorize my program to use it daily?* You need only to memorize or remember which activities you are using in your program. You should have your planner with you, and when you encounter the activities you can glean the key associations and self-suggestions written on it. You can either carry the book around with you, leaving a bookmark next to your current program planner, or you can extract your planner from the book (or photocopy it) so you carry with you only the pages you need. Most people discover, however, that after just a few days into their program, that they have automatically memorized the key associations and self-suggestions from their planner. When this happens, you no longer need to carry the book or planner with you.

7. *How do I evoke strong, positive emotions while performing the method?* One key to evoking the proper emotional state when putting the method into practice is to really think about the value and meaning of your selected activities as you perform them. Recognize the desire you have to improve yourself in your target area, and then let the emotions bubble up to the surface of your mind. It's important, however, not to force the emotion. Just focus on how much better your life will be when you've improved, and the emotion will follow.

8. *Is it effective to recite the self-suggestions more than once before performing an activity?* It can be. You can recite a self-suggestion up to three times before performing an activity from your program. More important than how many times you repeat it are the thoughts and emotions behind your words. Really connect with your drive to change yourself. If reciting the self-suggestions more than once helps you do that, by all means repeat it a few times. But you needn't ever go beyond a few repetitions.

## A Word from the Soapbox

By now, I hope you understand why the method disclosed is called Self-Hypnosis Revolution. Not only is it a revolutionary way to utilize the virtues of self-hypnosis without going into a trance, but it also offers a revolutionary way to view your life and personal growth on this planet. A Buddhist friend of mine, when I told him the basic premise this book, remarked that it reminded him of one of the tenants of his religion. To paraphrase, he told me that one of the markers of enlightenment on the Buddhist path is to experience joy in performing the simple tasks of life: to find bliss and meaning even while washing dishes or making a cup of tea. Now, while the benefits of the Self-Hypnosis Revolution method are geared toward practical self-improvement rather than spiritual enlightenment, it would certainly be a wonderful notion to think that you who read this work might experience joy and fulfillment from the ordinary tasks that constitute much of our waking lives.

I've considered whether the underlying significance I've discovered in common activities preexists or whether I've imposed it. For example, are the things we do everyday already full of meaning or are we artificially adding meaning to them? Either answer would have interesting psychological, philosophical, and even metaphysical implications. I've thought about it long and hard and I've come to no conclusion. In the end I guess it doesn't matter. As long as I can apply meaning and value in what I do, I'm content. Aren't you? And it's a marvelous realization that the so-called "small" things in life can matter. It suddenly puts the seemingly "big" activities of life into perspective. And I wonder which of the two kinds of activities (big or small) has a larger role in shaping what kind of person I am, what I believe, and what I really want from life. And that leads me to ask, "What makes one activity in life more important than another?"

I'll chew on that.

# Appendix A

More Ready-to-Go Programs

## Program Planner
## Target Area: Physical Wellness
## Start Date:
## End Date:

| Activity | Key Associations | Self-Suggestion |
|---|---|---|
| **1. Turning on a light** | Realization, knowledge, energy | "I light my way to complete physical health." |
| **2. Breathing** | Assimilation, release, life | "I draw life and energy into my body." |
| **3. Taking out the Trash** | Clearing, releasing, eliminating | "I efficiently eliminate from my body what it no longer uses for good health." |
| **4. Exercising** | Clearing, releasing, eliminating | "I use my effort to strengthen and heal my body." |
| **5. Cleaning** | Purification, order, maintenance | "I purify and maintain my body to be in perfect working order." |
| **6. Sleeping** | Restoration, processing | "My body repairs itself as I sleep and makes me stronger." |

*Do I want to continue this program for another seven-day cycle?*

_____yes _____no

Basic Technique Reminder

1. As you undertake each activity in daily life, review its key associations and recite with emotion the self-suggestion that corresponds with that activity.

2. Focus on each activity as you perform it while continuing to consider its key associations and symbolic meaning.

3. Perform the task with enthusiasm and interest, expecting positive changes in your life.

## Program Planner
**Target Area: Mental Wellness**
**Start Date:**
**End Date:**

| Activity | Key Associations | Self-Suggestion |
|---|---|---|
| **1. Awakening** | Realization, recognition | "I realize perfect balance in my thoughts and emotions." |
| **2. Brushing Teeth** | Maintaining power | "I purify my mind of fragmented thoughts to keep it strong and powerful." |
| **3. Drinking** | Satisfaction, emotions, spirituality, purification | "I satisfy my need for experiences that make me feel healthy and alive." |
| **4. Dressing** | Identity, self image | "I identify myself as someone who is mentally healthy and powerful." |
| **5. Home Improvement** | Self-improvement | "I enhance my emotional self and make improvements where needed." |
| **6. Shopping** | Searching, gathering, making choices | "I carefully choose for myself what to think and how to feel." |

1. *Do I want to continue this program for another seven-day cycle?*

_____yes _____no

Basic Technique Reminder

1. As you undertake each activity in daily life, review its key associations and recite with emotion the self-suggestion that corresponds with that activity.
2. Focus on each activity as you perform it while continuing to consider its key associations and symbolic meaning.
3. Perform the task with enthusiasm and interest, expecting positive changes in your life.

## Program Planner
**Target Area: Career and Finances**
**Start Date:**
**End Date:**

| Activity | Key Associations | Self-Suggestion |
|---|---|---|
| **1. Arriving** | Action, volition | "I arrive at my destination of success and abundance." |
| **2. Changing Linens** | Changing/purifying beliefs | "I change and purify self-protective beliefs about success and money." |
| **3. Plugging in Appliance** | Connection, power | "I connect with powerful ideas and people who empower my career and further my financial gain." |
| **4. Climbing Stairs** | Effort, achievement | "I recognize the steps required to reach my goals." |
| **5. Waiting** | Process, expectation, destiny | "I wait for and recognize opportunities for increased prosperity." |
| **6. Standing Up** | Recognition, self-assertion | "I stand up to voice my business acumen and ideas." |

*Do I want to continue this program for another seven-day cycle?*

_____yes _____no

Basic Technique Reminder
1. As you undertake each activity in daily life, review its key associations and recite with emotion the self-suggestion that corresponds with that activity.
2. Focus on each activity as you perform it while continuing to consider its key associations and symbolic meaning.
3. Perform the task with enthusiasm and interest, expecting positive changes in your life.

**Program Planner**
**Target Area: Relationships**
**Start Date:**
**End Date:**

| Activity | Key Associations | Self-Suggestion |
|---|---|---|
| 1. Ironing Clothes | Correcting, perfecting | "I iron out the challenges in my relationships that they may be harmonious and happy." |
| 2. Communicating | Understanding, information, rapport | "I accurately communicate with others and establish mutual understanding." |
| 3. Descending Stairs | Practicality, manifestation, effort | "I access deeper levels in my close relationships." |
| 4. Shopping | Searching, gathering, making choices | "I search for the best in all of my relationships." |
| 5. Unlocking a Door | Gaining access | "I unlock the door to my inner self to obtain honest, intimate relationships." |
| 6. Working | Effort for reward, service | "I make an effort and work toward excellent and loving relationships." |

*Do I want to continue this program for another seven-day cycle?*

_____yes _____no

Basic Technique Reminder
1. As you undertake each activity in daily life, review its key associations and recite with emotion the self-suggestion that corresponds with that activity.
2. Focus on each activity as you perform it while continuing to consider its key associations and symbolic meaning.
3. Perform the task with enthusiasm and interest, expecting positive changes in your life.

## Program Planner
**Target Area: Spirituality**
**Start Date:**
**End Date:**

| Activity | Key Associations | Self-Suggestion |
|---|---|---|
| **1. Unplugging an Appliance** | Discontinue, detachment | "I detach myself from any belief or behavior that is no longer of value in my spiritual development." |
| **2. Entering a Doorway** | Access, movement, initiation | "I walk through the doorway toward enlightenment." |
| **3. Changing a Light Bulb** | New ideas, understanding | "I replace burned-out ideas about the divine that no longer assist me for those that provide illumination to my soul." |
| **4. Pouring Liquid** | Expressing, channeling | "I channel love and desire into my spiritual activities." |
| **5. Computer Tasks** | Communication, programming | "The divine interfaces with me and upgrades my spiritual programming." |
| **6. Traveling** | Change, expansion | "I am on a spiritual journey that takes me toward my divine destination." |

*Do I want to continue this program for another seven-day cycle?*

_____yes _____no

Basic Technique Reminder
1. As you undertake each activity in daily life, review its key associations and recite with emotion the self-suggestion that corresponds with that activity.
2. Focus on each activity as you perform it while continuing to consider its key associations and symbolic meaning.
3. Perform the task with enthusiasm and interest, expecting positive changes in your life.

# Appendix B

## Blank Custom Program Planning Templates

## Your Custom Program Planning Template
**Target Area:**
**Start Date:**
**End Date:**

| Activity | Key Associations | Self-Suggestion |
|---|---|---|
| 1. | | |
| 2. | | |
| 3. | | |
| 4. | | |
| 5. | | |
| 6. | | |

*Do I want to continue this program for another seven-day cycle?*

_____yes _____no

Basic Technique Reminder

1. As you undertake each activity in daily life, review its key associations and recite with emotion the self-suggestion that corresponds with that activity.

2. Focus on each activity as you perform it while continuing to consider its key associations and symbolic meaning.

3. Perform the task with enthusiasm and interest, expecting positive changes in your life.

## Your Custom Program Planning Template
**Target Area:**
**Start Date:**
**End Date:**

| Activity | Key Associations | Self-Suggestion |
|---|---|---|
| 1. | | |
| 2. | | |
| 3. | | |
| 4. | | |
| 5. | | |
| 6. | | |

*Do I want to continue this program for another seven-day cycle?*

____yes ____no

Basic Technique Reminder

1. As you undertake each activity in daily life, review its key associations and recite with emotion the self-suggestion that corresponds with that activity.

2. Focus on each activity as you perform it while continuing to consider its key associations and symbolic meaning.

3. Perform the task with enthusiasm and interest, expecting positive changes in your life.

## Your Custom Program Planning Template
**Target Area:**
**Start Date:**
**End Date:**

| Activity | Key Associations | Self-Suggestion |
|---|---|---|
| 1. | | |
| 2. | | |
| 3. | | |
| 4. | | |
| 5. | | |
| 6. | | |

*Do I want to continue this program for another seven-day cycle?*

_____yes _____no

Basic Technique Reminder

1. As you undertake each activity in daily life, review its key associations and recite with emotion the self-suggestion that corresponds with that activity.

2. Focus on each activity as you perform it while continuing to consider its key associations and symbolic meaning.

3. Perform the task with enthusiasm and interest, expecting positive changes in your life.

**Your Custom Program Planning Template**
**Target Area:**
**Start Date:**
**End Date:**

| Activity | Key Associations | Self-Suggestion |
|---|---|---|
| 1. | | |
| 2. | | |
| 3. | | |
| 4. | | |
| 5. | | |
| 6. | | |

*Do I want to continue this program for another seven-day cycle?*

_____yes _____no

Basic Technique Reminder

1. As you undertake each activity in daily life, review its key associations and recite with emotion the self-suggestion that corresponds with that activity.
2. Focus on each activity as you perform it while continuing to consider its key associations and symbolic meaning.
3. Perform the task with enthusiasm and interest, expecting positive changes in your life.

## Your Custom Program Planning Template
**Target Area:**
**Start Date:**
**End Date:**

| Activity | Key Associations | Self-Suggestion |
|---|---|---|
| 1. | | |
| 2. | | |
| 3. | | |
| 4. | | |
| 5. | | |
| 6. | | |

*Do I want to continue this program for another seven-day cycle?*
\_\_\_\_yes \_\_\_\_no

Basic Technique Reminder
1. As you undertake each activity in daily life, review its key associations and recite with emotion the self-suggestion that corresponds with that activity.
2. Focus on each activity as you perform it while continuing to consider its key associations and symbolic meaning.
3. Perform the task with enthusiasm and interest, expecting positive changes in your life.

**Your Custom Program Planning Template**
**Target Area:**
**Start Date:**
**End Date:**

| Activity | Key Associations | Self-Suggestion |
|---|---|---|
| 1. | | |
| 2. | | |
| 3. | | |
| 4. | | |
| 5. | | |
| 6. | | |

*Do I want to continue this program for another seven-day cycle?*

_____yes _____no

Basic Technique Reminder

1. As you undertake each activity in daily life, review its key associations and recite with emotion the self-suggestion that corresponds with that activity.
2. Focus on each activity as you perform it while continuing to consider its key associations and symbolic meaning.
3. Perform the task with enthusiasm and interest, expecting positive changes in your life.

# Index of Activities

Activities

Activities

Activities

Activities

# About the Author

**F**orbes Robbins Blair runs his own self-empowerment business called New Creations, which he began in 1990. He is the author of the bestselling *Instant Self-Hypnosis: How to Hypnotize Yourself with Your Eyes Open*. He graduated from the University of Maryland and received a bachelor of arts degree in radio, TV, and film. He became a professional clinical hypnotherapist in 1997 after receiving certification from the American Institute of Hypnotherapy in 1996. Forbes is also a dream coach and analyst and facilitates dream groups. He teaches classes on dream analysis, self-hypnosis, astral travel, ghost detection, and Western mysticism. He has appeared on television and national radio for his expertise in both hypnosis and dream analysis. Forbes lives in Silver Spring, Maryland, and can be reached through his website: www.ForbesRobbinsBlair.com.